The Connected Consumer

The Connected Consumer

Dinesh Kumar

BUSINESS EXPERT PRESS

The Connected Consumer

First published in 2016 by
Business Expert Press, LLC
222 East 46th Street, New York, NY 10017
www.businessexpertpress.com

ISBN-13: 978-1-63157-110-7 (paperback)
ISBN-13: 978-1-63157-111-4 (e-book)

Business Expert Press Digital and Social Media Marketing and Advertising Collection

Collection ISSN: 2333-8822 (print)
Collection ISSN: 2333-8830 (electronic)

Cover and interior design by Exeter Premedia Services Private Ltd., Chennai, India

First edition: 2016

10 9 8 7 6 5 4 3 2 1

Printed in the United States of America.

Abstract

Traditional marketing faces challenges as never before. The way that people interact with each other and with companies is changing completely in today's era of 24/7 connectivity. This book explores tectonic changes in buyer behavior and how businesses are responding to those changes. It describes how data is used to track and analyze customers in almost everything they do, and how marketing communications are delivered with precision to individual mobile devices. The connected customer is blurring the line between online and offline sales resulting in an entirely new purchase cycle.

The "always on" consumer has ushered in an era of customer engagement. In developed countries, online commerce offers limitless ease and variety for customers, while in developing countries e-commerce and e-finance provides access for millions of people to formal banking channels and also to empower them.

Companies are merging their online and offline business models. While data is being used to analyze and track customers, at the same time it raises a worrying question—does this constant peering into customers' lives has limits? Will it result in a consumer utopia or a privacy nightmare?

This book helps understand how consumers and companies are changing, leading to profound changes in marketing.

Keywords

consumer behavior, connected consumer, consumer decision journey, data analytics, digital marketing, e-commerce, financial inclusion, marketing

Contents

Acknowledgments

Many people have helped me in writing this book. I would like to thank all of them.

My family members who have been a constant support in my endeavors, offering help and advice at every stage.

My colleagues, who have always been a source of support and inspiration.

IBM and McKinsey, who were very kind to grant permission to use two crucial exhibits in this book.

Dr Victoria L. Crittenden, Professor & Chair, Marketing Division, Babson College, for giving me an opportunity to write this book.

CHAPTER 1

Traditional Marketing Faces a Challenge Today

Mary is a bright young girl born at the turn of the century, who loves her phone. She uses it for a number of things and checks it every few minutes. It is an addiction. Young people like Mary can't do without 24/7 connectivity and their behavior is changing because of that. Consequently, how they search and buy things is changing too. The traditional marketing model no longer works and businesses have to change in response to tectonic changes in human behavior. Companies have to cater to a growing population of connected consumers like Mary, and we follow her in this book, discovering the huge changes that she and people like her are causing. In this chapter, we look at changes in the way that companies will do business.

There was a time, not very long ago, when companies relied on similar marketing methods to get their idea across to consumers. Newspapers and television carried ads into people's homes. The daily dose of entertainment and news also slipped in advertisements that showed beautiful people using those products and living happily ever after. Then the companies waited as people rushed to stores to buy their soaps and lotions and the great things that had made the people so wonderful and happy.

Marketing consisted of periodically *spraying* consumers with advertising in the manner of using sprays on insects: The *spray and pray* strategy worked for a while, after which the little things got immune and newer sprays had to be invented. Consumers similarly got immune after a while and then newer ways of persuading them had to be found.

The advertising *sprays* worked for many years, riding on the power of mass media. But then, the media started fragmenting. Channels and newspapers multiplied. Marketing managers did not know who was watching what. The invention of the remote control further spoiled the traditional model: It gave consumers the power to zap advertisements. Companies were losing the means to reach their customers.

This was not all.

The IT industry then reduced the size of computers and placed them on people's laps. People could now choose what they wanted to watch and when, rather than depend on TV channels or newspapers. Mobile phones further put small screens in the hands of people which they could carry wherever they went. Consumers no longer relied on mass media now, but could watch or read anything, anywhere. The marriage of mobiles and IT gave more power to consumers—they could do much more now—connect with friends, post comments and reviews, engage with brands, or tell them off, even while doing many other things (Exhibit 1.1).

Exhibit 1.1

A Day in Mary's Life

Mary wakes up, gets ready for work, and hurries to the subway station. At the gates, she swipes her watch at the turnstile, which reads the code on it and the gates open for her. In the train, she remembers she has to buy groceries, she needs a new dress, and a beep on the phone tells her that the birthday of a friend is approaching. She settles down on her seat and uses her phone to place an order for groceries on a site she trusts. It already has a shopping list based on her past purchases and all she has to do is tick whatever she needs. Payment is made seamlessly by pressing her thumb print on the screen.

Next she decides to look for a dress and browses several of them. When she gets down from the train, she grabs a coffee from a kiosk and pays by swiping her watch. A screen at the kiosk displays dresses similar to the one she is searching. One of them catches her eye and she takes a picture of the Quick Response (QR) code on her phone.

At work, she is busy in the morning; but when she is free, she tries the dresses she had browsed earlier on a virtual model that looks like her. When she shortlists some, she sends it to her friends for their opinions. Her friends immediately respond with their comments and also send her links to reviews that others have posted.

After office, she goes to her favorite store to try out some dresses. The store manager greets her by name and shows her dresses on 3-D displays and virtual models. Her friend, who has tracked her through an app, walks in and the two girls look and select a dress.

Unfortunately, the dress that she selects is not available in her size. The store manager uses his tablet to see if it is available in another store. An order is placed.

By the time she gets home, her groceries have been delivered. Soon a drone arrives with her dress and she excitedly tries it on.

Tectonic Changes

This represents a tectonic change in human behavior as never before. Consequently, companies have had to make changes in the way they make marketing plans because the traditional ways of communicating with and engaging people have changed (Figure 1.1). The smartphone has changed the way we go about our lives in many ways as follows:

- People access information about anything, anytime.
- They post pictures and videos about themselves and what they experience.

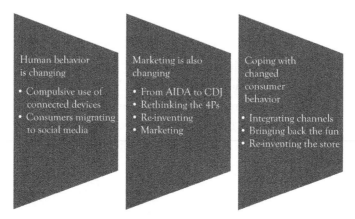

Figure 1.1 Changes in human behavior are forcing marketing to change, which in turn is inducing change in the ways of doing business

- People connect with their friends, strangers, and companies at the click of a button.
- Things are bought and sold with ease, and a sharing economy is also taking shape.
- Apps allow people to do a variety of things on the devices.

Frelin (2013) writes, "Digital has resulted in profound shifts in the business of marketing, with innovation dramatically increasing the ability to target and engage with consumers." Apps allow customers and companies to interact with each other in progressively better ways.

People are giving mass media the go-by and are instead perpetually using their mobile devices or checking them: It has become an addiction. A report by Flurry Analytics says that an average mobile user launches an app 10 times per day, but a mobile addict launches them more than 60 times each day. By tracking 500,000 apps on 1.3 billion mobile devices, Flurry has deduced that the number of mobile addicts grew from 79 million people to 176 million people between March 2013 and March 2014—an increase of 123 percent.

Another study reported in *Time* (2014) says that 73 percent people admit to feeling panicky if they misplace their phone. Many users exhibit compulsive behavior: They feel the urge to check up their phones every few minutes. About 25 percent mobile phone users admit to checking their phones while driving. Smartphones are changing human behavior in many ways. The study found that:

- Nearly 60 percent of smartphone owners do not go an hour without checking their phones.
- Some 54 percent check their phones while in bed—before they go to sleep, after they wake up, or in the middle of the night. Also, one in five checks immediately after sex.
- Nearly 40 percent check their phones while on the toilet.
- Some 30 percent check their phones during a meal with others, and 9 percent check their phones during religious services.

All this requires a change in approach by the marketing managers. Companies realize that they have to modify their strategies to align with the changing aspects of human behavior. They have to get a foothold in consumers' minds even as they do things on their mobile phones and other connected devices.

They face several questions. How are they going to *spray* the customers with marketing when nobody knows what channels they are using? How are they to reach customers with their lovely ads and the sales pitches?

So, is traditional marketing dead? Do we need to reinvent our thinking?

Several business thinkers have echoed this thought. Indeed, traditional marketing faces a challenge in trying to understand consumer behavior in the era of digital marketing. Lee (2012) writes that traditional marketing methods are dead, because consumer habits have changed. He points to a paradigm shift in consumer behavior: Rather than encourage customer advocacy with cash rewards and inducements, the new marketing tries to create social capital through affiliation networks and gives them access to new knowledge. The decline of traditional marketing has been due to the following causes:

- Buyers do not pay attention to marketing messages in the mass media.
- Mass media has fragmented.
- CEOs do not trust that marketing spends will bring in results.
- Traditional marketing and sales pitches do not work today.

In a connected, data-abundant world, customers are unlikely to be swayed by sales pitches. Now they are online most of the time, at home, in office, and even while traveling. Companies, which earlier relied on mass media to reach customers, have no option but to follow their customers online. But this is easier said than done: Any intrusion by a company into personal virtual lives is not welcome, and will be blocked out or severely punished. So, companies have to devise ways to fit in with what people are doing online. That is why they have to understand contemporary culture, which is changing today because of the following four factors (Rob Fields, 2014):

1. *Social media*: People love social media, checking it out compulsively, sometimes several times a day. Sites like Twitter, Facebook, LinkedIn, and Google+ show us what customers are interested in and also

contain a wealth of personal data. So, how is that to be used in marketing?

2. *The human business movement:* People do not like to be talked down to, but engage with corporations. When they feel interested, they will contribute to business in a variety of ways. This gives rise to two challenges: first, companies have to engage their audiences and second, they have to learn to be transparent and communicate in a simple, straightforward manner.

3. *The purpose economy:* Consumers look not only for products and brands, but also to solve problems. This has resulted in the rise of the sharing economy, in which things like cars, rooms, or bicycles are rented out to people who need them through apps. A peer-to-peer review system allows people on both sides to assess their customers and buyers. Consumers look for opportunities to work with companies and organizations that bring value to their lives and to society.

4. *Rethinking the organization:* These massive changes are forcing a rethink on the business organization. Today brands and communications are owned by people, not companies. The top-down marketing that we are all familiar with no longer exists. Chief Marketing Officers have to evolve into Chief Experience Officers.

This means that the old ways of marketing certainly require a rethink. Companies have to find ways as to what works in the new environment and what does not.

So What Works?

The new marketing must gear toward peer influence, community-oriented marketing, and customer relationships. As Pearson (2011) explains, "The fundamentals have changed, as have the means and methods to define targets, to create more productive encounters that provide more opportunities to sell, to develop deeper and more significant insights, and to exploit singular points of difference."

The problem is that in the online world, companies no longer control marketing stimuli. People choose their own content themselves and are quick to avoid overtly commercial messages they are not interested in. They are having love affairs with their phones and do not want any undesired intrusions in their personal space. This makes the task of companies quite difficult, as they now have to find out how best to make the consumer interested and how to design sales pitches to them.

Digital strategy has to ensure that product messages are where the consumer is, that is, on their mobile devices. But since people do not like to be disturbed when they are doing things on their devices, companies have to look for ways to leverage social media presence, or provide interesting apps or content that *makes the customer want to engage with the brand*. The challenge is to get a foothold in consumers' minds as they browse and interact with others online. This is easier said than done, of course, since people dislike spam and are quick to block unwanted messages and calls.

Understanding today's consumer behavior involves finding out:

- What the consumer is browsing
- What type of channel do consumers prefer
- What type of products appeals to consumers
- What drives consumers online and what are their habits
- What are the factors affecting online purchases
- What gets people talking about products and brands

Consumer behavior study reveals that people are not buying the way they used to—by narrowing choices as they went along—but embark on journeys of discovery, discussion, purchase, and advocacy.

Consumer Decision Journey

Online consumers buy differently. Today the consumer decision-making process is more likely to be explained through the consumer decision journey (CDJ).

Traditional marketing has depended on the purchase funnel to understand consumer behavior. According to this, the consumer moves over four stages when exposed to marketing stimuli and is explained by the AIDA model. First people become aware of a product or brand, which is followed by interest and desire, and finally action, or the purchase decision. This is logical, of course, since the customer starts with a broad range of choices and gradually narrows them down. A large number of people become aware due to marketing activities, but progressively fewer numbers remain interested and fewer still actually buy the product. It is a linear model, represented by a funnel that keeps getting narrow as people move from one stage to the next.

Today people do not move in a straight, linear path from one stage to the next. They look for information from multiple sources, seeking advice from their friends, checking out opinions of others online, and interacting with friends, companies, and media at every stage of the purchase process. The decision-making process is thus more complex and can change at every stage.

A consumer's purchase path today usually begins with the consumer getting influenced by someone, going online to search and talk about it, and getting information or reviews. In this new purchasing behavior, companies must set up digital interactions at all stages, right from the intention to purchase to the postpurchase stage. The process, called the CDJ, is shown in Figure 1.2.

The concept was developed after examining the purchase decisions of 20,000 consumers by McKinsey. Its authors Court et al. (2009) write, "CDJ combines all elements of marketing—strategy, spending, channel management, and message—with the journey that consumers undertake when they make purchasing decisions but also of integrating those elements across the organization."

The CDJ shows that there are many influences on the consumer before the decision-making process, and these do not proceed step by step.

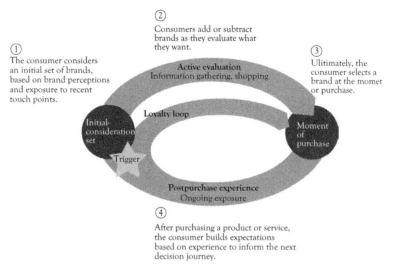

② Consumers add or subtract brands as they evaluate what they want.

① The consumer considers an initial set of brands, based on brand perceptions and exposure to recent touch points.

③ Ultimately, the consumer selects a brand at the momet or purchase.

Active evaluation
Information gathering, shopping

Loyalty loop

Initial-consideration set

Moment of purchase

Trigger

Postpurchase experience
Ongoing exposure

④ After purchasing a product or service, the consumer builds expectations based on experience to inform the next decision journey.

Figure 1.2 The consumer decision journey

People do not depend on one-way communication from the mass media any more, but use many different sources of information. It is a two-way conversation now, and companies have to satisfy customer demands for transparency and information and also manage word-of-mouth (WOM) interactions.

The consumer decision-making process has become more like a circular journey with four primary phases: consider, evaluate, buy, and experience. Edelman (2010) further explains the last stage as enjoy, advocate, and bond. The last stage is important as consumers will bring others to the fold by sharing and broadcasting their positive experiences. The new CDJ can be summed up as CEPEA—consider, evaluate, purchase, enjoy, and advocate. Companies have to build their strategy around consumer experience planning (CEP) that delivers the brand promise coherently and consistently along touch points of the CEPEA journey, as explained below.

> *Consider:* The CDJ begins with products that a person is aware of, or the consideration set. Earlier, this set contained a large number of brands, but today's consumers have reduced the number of

products they consider. They are guided by ads or store displays, but more importantly, by recommendations of friends or someone they know and trust.

Evaluate: Next, they seek advice and inputs from a variety of online and offline interactions with peers, reviewers, retailers, friends, the brand, and its competitors. New brands are added to the set and some are discarded. The two-way communication is part of the evaluation process.

Buy: Before they buy, people like to check out products in a store. They like to see and feel the product, its packaging, and enjoy the purchase experience. The physical purchase may be made online or offline, but each element at the point of purchase is important and can result in acceptance or rejection of the product.

Enjoy, advocate, bond: After buying, people like to enjoy the product, talk about it, and bond with people who feel the same way. It is a crucial step in the consumption cycle, which is ignored by the purchase funnel analogy. They develop a deeper connection as they experience the product and share their experience with others. Many consumers, in fact, conduct online research about the products after the purchase. If they are pleased, they post positive reviews, share it with friends, and advocate the product or brand, contributing to WOM publicity. Conversely, a bad experience is also broadcast instantly.

There are two implications of this.

- First, traditional marketing efforts are not directed at the touch points at which the consumers are best influenced; mostly they are directed at advertising and point-of-purchase promotions. The CDJ recognizes that consumers are often influenced by somebody else's experience and later, they like to tell others. These two stages are crucial and companies have to invest in the experience stage as well.

- Second, companies have to invest in two-way communication by using owned media and earned media. *Owned media* is what is controlled by the company, that is, advertisements, promotions, websites, and such. *Earned media* consists of channels not controlled by the company, including online review sites, social media, blogs, and sites which give voice to the customer.

The CDJ and the digital transformation also impact the way that customer value is created.

Customer Value Creation

Customer value is created by using all the characteristics of the digital interaction. Pine and Korn (2011) describe a *multiverse* which reshapes the landscape by altering three dimensions—time, no-space, and no-matter. Technology extends each of these dimensions for value creation:

- *Time*: Today's customers interact with companies through nonlinear, asynchronous methods. That is, they want to do business when they feel like. They will interact with a company when it fits their own schedule, rather than matching with the company's opening and closing times. This means that a company must be responsive at all times.
- *No-space*: Digital technology enables companies to construct offerings in virtual places rather than in real places. Companies can interact with customers on websites, via social media, in virtual worlds, on whatever device best meets their individual needs. This enables them to enter the virtual world of customers.
- *No-matter*: Offerings need no longer be composed merely of material substances, but can also be formed digitally. Companies have to be digitally oriented, integrating the advantages of being offline and online to their offerings to meet the demands of the connected consumer.

Companies have, therefore, to fuse the real and the virtual worlds the same way that customers do. They do this in various ways. Courier companies let customers track packages through their websites. Restaurants enhance their real places with Wi-Fi access. Apparel retailers help people try out new clothes on virtual models and help them select what suits them best. Some companies that have used digital value creation in their business models are described in Exhibit 1.2 that follows.

Exhibit 1.2
Digital Value Creators

Some amazing and unique businesses have resulted because of digital value creation. Others have transformed themselves to be more relevant to their customers. Take a look at some of the successful companies:

Airbnb: Airbnb helps people rent out rooms; customers get lower rates than a hotel would charge, while the owner makes some extra money. "We verify personal profiles and listings, maintain a smart messaging system, so hosts and guests can communicate with certainty, and manage a trusted platform to collect and transfer payments," says its website.

Starbucks: Starbucks' app is an easy-to-use payment and loyalty card, and helps customers find location of Starbucks stores in unfamiliar cities. It also provides *pick of the week* music to keep people entertained while they are waiting in line. The company realizes that the app is about *relationships, not marketing.*

Krispy Kreme: The store has a *HOT Doughnuts Now* light that lets customers know when hot doughnuts come off the line. Now the company connects that light to the Internet through an app: It alerts customers when hot doughnuts are being made at a store near them. The company found its Hot Light app more powerful than placing ads in traditional media.

The lesson from these companies is that companies have to be more focused on their customers and their purchase journeys. They have to find out customer problem and solve them through the connected device. Only then will customers respond to the companies' marketing efforts.

These companies show that the digital invasion is an opportunity to add value to a firm's current offerings. Some companies do so by offering online services like Google and Facebook. Others use the Internet as a distribution channel, selling software and music. Many other companies use it as an electronic store. New opportunities are being created. According to McKinsey (2012), connected consumers give rise to three key trends in digital business—big data and analytics, digital marketing and social-media tools, and the use of new delivery platforms such as cloud computing and mobility. The report says that though there are high expectations of value generation because of this, many companies were not ready to meet the challenges created by these trends.

However, companies can create value for the customer using the tools and technologies available easily today. The Internet offers a way to talk to and track customers as one-to-one marketing evolves. This leads us to rethinking the four Ps of marketing.

Rethinking the Four Ps

It is clear that conventional thinking on marketing will not work in the new digital realities. It is time to rethink the basics of marketing to serve connected customers. Webster and Lusch (2013) say that a new marketing concept is emerging that must keep into account the following:

1. *Customer-defined value*: Companies have to shift to creating customer-defined value, replacing the old concept of manufacturer-controlled production.
2. *Citizen-consumer*: The customer is seen in a set of relationships over multiple subsystems, and is involved in co-creating customer-defined value.
3. *New value propositions*: Companies have to continuously improve and offer new value propositions, supported by processes to be able to engage with customers.
4. *Adaptive organization*: Marketing organizations will have to be adaptive to defend against threats and create new markets or submarkets.
5. *Educating customers*: Companies have to educate, not just inform, potential customers. This involves knowing customers and sharing of knowledge with them.

Ettenson, Conrado, and Knowles (2013) suggest that the four Ps of marketing can be thought of as shifting the emphasis from products to solutions, place to access, price to value, and promotion to education (solutions, access, value, and education, SAVE). The focus of marketing as given by this model is summed up below:

- *From product to solution*: Today, customers expect *solutions*. These are offered through customized products and services. Thus, companies have to focus on how their products make lives easier for their customers. That is, they take a customer-centric approach and see why consumers use each product and which problem is solved by it.
- *From place to access*: The focus is no longer on individual purchases at a location, but *access*. Customers expect easy and 24/7 access, so companies have to develop an integrated omnichannel that consumers can access, based on the entire purchase journey of the consumer.
- *From price to value*: Instead of focusing on price, as it related to production and manufacturing and distribution costs, companies must learn to associate benefits delivered relative to the price. They must think of ways to deliver *value* to their customers.
- *From promotion to education*: Traditionally companies have relied on advertising, PR, and personal selling. In the new orientation, they have to provide specific information at each stage of the CDJ. Instead of promoting products, companies have to focus on providing information and *education*.

Such a shift in thinking is required to enhance customer experience across channels. The basics of marketing need a change, as summarized in Table 1.1.

While companies respond to changing behavior by modifying their approach to marketing, many traditional businesses and bricks-and-mortar retailing companies feel threatened—and rightly so. Sales volumes in physical stores have declined in many countries as volumes of

Table 1.1 Online consumer behavior and marketing strategy

Product	Individualized and augmented products Digital products and services Products not carried in inventory in physical stores Get over the limitations of space and offer unlimited product choices online
Price	Offer value to customers and make their lives easier Easy comparison of prices, cash on delivery facilities Deals and discounts; tie-up with banks and easy payments Algorithm-based pricing based on supply and demand
Place	Quick and continuous access through virtual shop fronts, interactive displays Try and buy facilities Real-time inventory tracking across channels and delivery
Promotion	Educate customers by providing complete information Encourage WOM publicity, C2C communications Focused promotional messages rather than annoying people Multichannel promotion, integration of online and offline messages
People	Trained store and delivery personnel with online access Absence of pushy salespersons; trained salespersons with tablets Advice and support online through chat and other means Automated processes and customer service
Physical evidence	Website design, on-site assurance, refund policies Independent reviews, *try and buy* facilities Physical stores augmenting online experience
Process	Quick order-taking, delivery, tracking, and delivery processes Transactional and internal communications Integration of business processes

online merchants have skyrocketed (see Chapter 2). Many businesses—travel agents, music and book stores, brokerages, and the like—have been sucked in by online portals. Businesses that thrived by leveraging scarce information have suddenly become extinct. Companies today need strategies for coping with these tectonic changes.

Coping with Change

Change is coming faster than expected, and companies are trying to cope with changes in consumer behavior in a variety of ways.

Businesses, big and small, have to learn to do business in times of perfect information. Rather than fight something that cannot be stopped, they have to learn to use the new technologies to help in their businesses. In fact, online technologies open up a host of opportunities through the following:

- *Remote store fronts*: Remote store fronts are displayed at subway stations or at places that people frequent. People use these store fronts to scan QR codes with their smartphones and have the products delivered to their homes, sometimes on the same day.
- *Discounts and deals*: Smartphones are being used to make consumers aware of discounts or special deals and to connect them with additional product information that will help them make purchase decisions.
- *Trained staff*: Physical stores offer consultancy and advice through trained staff armed with tablets. Knowledgeable and skilled in-store sales associates make for superior customer service experiences.
- *Touch-and-feel factor*: Many retailers try to capitalize on the touch-and-feel factor. Since consumers shopping for expensive gadgets or apparel like to touch and feel them before buying, they try to improve customer experience and get families into stores. This is done by enhancing in-store ambience with a bright and rich display of products and integrating the digital and offline worlds. Lounges, in which customers interact with trained sales staff or *tech buddies*, are seen in many stores.
- *Integrate online and offline*: Integrating online and offline stores and offering consumers the options to shop online and collect from any of its offline stores, or shopping at offline stores and accessing service and support on online portals are ways to deliver customer satisfaction.
- *Using technology and apps*: Retailers are now introducing apps, mobile-shopping tools, and online features that mimic show rooming (Chapter 3).

- *Locating customers*: Using GPS technology, the apps on smartphones can determine the location of each customer. The Guardian Media Network Blog (2013) reports that using Bluetooth technology, stores can now pinpoint customers within 2 cm. Apple uses iBeacon which is used in its own stores and other stores. As a customer comes near a store or a particular shelf in a supermarket, the app sends special offers on his or her smartphone. Consumer behavior can also be monitored, as these devices are able to track all movements of customers. By integrating data from reward programs and customer relationship management (CRM) initiatives, companies are able to get deep insight into the shopping habits of customers (Exhibit 1.3).

Exhibit 1.3

Changing Retail

Walmart has added its *In-Store Mode* to its iPhone app. Consumers who launch the app in a Walmart store can scan the bar codes for price checks, customer reviews, and information about the product. The app also helps consumers in accessing the latest ads, discounts, and QR codes, which help lower the prices listed in the store.

Similarly, Target shoppers can use the *Shopkick* app, through which consumers earn points, or *kicks*, by scanning merchandise in the store. The kicks can be redeemed for things like gift cards and iTunes downloads. Target hopes that people who scan the goods will be more likely to buy those goods in the store.

Best Buy allows customers to shop online in stores, even if they do not have mobile devices. Salespeople equipped with tablets and other devices help shoppers find more detail on the products and look up reviews while in the Best Buy store.

The grocery chain Safeway introduced the *Just 4 U* digital savings program at its stores, which sends personalized deals to shoppers when they are in the store. Such deals make customers buy from the store immediately rather than waiting to compare prices elsewhere.

Another factor that underlies online shopping is the element of fun. Customers like to share their searches with friends, post pictures with their products on social sites, and enjoy getting *liked*, and discuss and seek opinions. The High Street, on the other hand, has attracted people because it is fun to go out with friends. Can brick-and-mortar stores bring back the fun into shopping?

Bringing Back the Fun

Retail companies try to bring back the fun into the shopping experience as a means to get customers into stores. Shopping for fashion and some expensive items has traditionally been a social activity: People like to hang out with their family or friends, eat together, and share experiences. Global shopping malls are trying to bring back the social and fun experience into shopping as a means of countering online buying.

The experience that people had on the shopping street is sought to be replaced by online search for bargains and social sharing in online buying. Clifford (2012) reports how Glimcher Realty Trust, which owns and manages shopping malls in the United States, is trying to make the malls fun by leasing out space to businesses that do more than sell stuff. By adding shops offering laser salons, giving hairstyling lessons, and teaching clay modeling, it hopes to bring the social experience and wean customers to shop as well. The idea is to involve people in fun activities like getting their hair done, or making pottery, soap, or a cake, with their friends.

As a result, shoppers in the United States will find such businesses in malls:

- *Make meaning*—A membership store where people make crafts, cakes, and other things
- *Drybar*—A salon with no scissors, just stylists with blow-dryers, so that shoppers can have their hair blown into beachy waves
- *Blissful yoga*—A service that offers yoga lessons
- *Industrie Denim*—A jeans store where women can study their rear view by a *booty cam*
- *Lego store*—A store that offers Lego-construction classes

Managers have realized that shopping malls would not work by themselves, and had to look for game-changing approaches. So, a number of add-ons are being offered, so that consumers get opportunities to do something meaningful, giving them a reason to visit the mall. Concept stores offering the experience often help in sales of other stores in the mall as well.

Aubrey and Judge (2012) write that far from sounding the death knell for the physical store, the new environment opens an opportunity for brands with bricks-and-mortar retail stores. Brands and stores have to reinvent themselves so that they deliver on four fronts: experience, service, consumer-focused logistics, and integration into its omnichannel system. Indeed, connectivity is having a cascading effect on businesses.

Cascading Effects

As bricks-and-mortar companies face up to changed realities, e-commerce companies have found 24/7 connectivity a boon. We explore the boom in e-commerce in Chapter 2. The buying behavior of customers like Mary is discovered in Chapter 3. Little does she know, but Mary and her tribe are forcing companies to change, affecting the marketing organization of the future, which is explored in Chapter 4. How companies track Mary through powerful tools such as data mining and analytics is explained in Chapter 5. Mary does not read newspapers, and how marketing communications and advertising are getting impacted is described in Chapter 6, while the tools to measure marketing ROI are described in Chapter 7. Finally, we attempt to see where we are heading and describe future scenarios in Chapter 8.

The rules of traditional marketing are being rewritten, as this chapter shows. But what we are seeing is a transition phase. In an interview with McKinsey (2013), Cisco's Chief Technology and Strategy Officer Padmasree Warrior said, "Today only 1 percent of what can be connected in the world is actually connected." That is, there is a lot more that will be connected in the times to come. The constant connectivity is, of course, a boon for e-commerce companies, who use it to sell products.

CHAPTER 2

The Age of E-commerce

Mary loves to shop. Easy access, limitless variety, easy payments—online connectivity has been a blessing both for consumers and online companies. Consumers like Mary are the engines of e-commerce, which has grown exponentially in many countries. Omnichannel business is a reality, and in poor countries, connectivity has meant bringing millions of disadvantaged people into the mainstream.

As people spend most of their lives fiddling with their connected devices, it was only natural that commerce moved there as well. People love to try out and buy new things. In the age of e-commerce, they get the means to do so at their finger tips. The long commute, the wait, and even the monotony of fiddling with online devices—all can be broken by browsing the huge variety of new products that are so easily accessible. Who can resist taking a look at the latest gadget or that little dress when it is so easy to do it? Today, thanks to easy connectivity, availability of payment gateways and systems to ease the buying process, e-commerce has grown considerably all over the globe. The Forrester Research Online Forecast (Sehgal 2013) says that e-commerce accounted for almost 9 percent of the $3.2 trillion total retail market in 2013 and is expected to grow at a compound annual growth rate of 10 percent between 2013 and 2018.

The phenomenon is not limited to the United States alone. The e-commerce sales in Western Europe is expected to grow at an even faster rate than in the United States in the next five years, from €112 billion in 2012 to €191 billion by 2017, representing a compound annual growth rate of 11 percent. In the UK, online retail already accounts for 13 percent of the total economy, and is expected to increase its share to 15 percent in 2017, according to the report. The IBM Retail 2020 (2012) report says that e-commerce is growing at five times the rate of traditional retailing and is expected to be over $500 billion within the decade.

Developing countries too are showing sizeable increase in online purchasing. China's e-commerce market was estimated to be $210 billion in 2012, growing at a phenomenal compound annual growth rate of 120 percent since 2003, according to a report by McKinsey Global Institute (2013). The e-tail had a share of about 5 to 6 percent of total retail sales in 2012. Indian e-commerce has grown at a compounded annual growth rate of 30 percent since 2009, and is one of the fastest growing online markets. It is estimated to be $16 billion in 2015, growing to $50 billion by 2020, according to a report in *Business Standard* (2015).

Connected Devices and E-commerce

Digital devices have invaded our lives. People have come to love their smartphones. They see the phone as a device that helps them in many ways. This gives enormous opportunity to companies to plug in their content that interests users and leads them to their products and brands. E-commerce gets a huge boost from smartphone ubiquity.

Many factors have contributed to the growth of e-commerce. Among them are:

- A growing pool of technology-savvy population;
- Exponential growth of mobile phones and Internet penetration;
- Increased comfort with the use of electronic payments through credit and debit cards;
- Developing countries catching up in consumption with the rest of the world;
- Rapid spread of social media, increasing brand awareness;
- Offline stores selling online as well; and
- Micro payments, which help the poor to bank and transact.

Market estimates by Gartner (2014) show that the devices are indeed becoming popular: Worldwide, smartphones have been selling more than basic feature phones since 2013. It says that the share is increasing as prices of smartphones drop. A screen in every hand has changed the buying habits and has helped developing countries to leapfrog into a connected world (Figure 2.1).

Figure 2.1 How the always-on customer is causing the push to omnichannel retail in the rich world and financial inclusion in the developing nations

A Surfeit of Screens

Screens have become ubiquitous. Research conducted by Vivaldi Partners (2014) shows that people in the United States use three connected devices every day, get online multiple times a day, and do so from at least three different locations. The study shows that 48 percent of consumers today are *Always-On* consumers who are obsessed with staying connected, leading to huge changes in human behavior. When asked what they would forgo for a year to be able to maintain Internet access, the study reports that:

- About 7 percent of U.S. consumers said they would forgo showering for a year;
- 21 percent said they would give up sex; and
- 73 percent said they would sacrifice alcohol.

This has resulted in a shift in media consumption patterns. A report by Nielsen, *The Digital Consumer* (2014) finds that consumption of TV content has increased because of the ability to watch time-shifted content. While watching TV, people also use their smartphones and tablets, using their devices as second-screens. This opens many avenues to deepen engagement with customers—an ad watched on TV can be immediately supplemented with information on the connected device, with the ability to order and pay at once.

Social media also helps e-commerce as it has become ingrained into the lives of consumers. By being present on such sites, a huge opportunity exists for the companies to increase their exposure with consumers during their consumer decision journeys. It is hardly a wonder that mobile retail is gaining momentum, with a huge majority of U.S. smartphone and tablet owners using a mobile device for shopping; developing countries, lagging basic telephony services, are leapfrogging to mobile transactions. Using a combination of media, including TV and online devices, companies find opportunities to reach customers at all times. Companies find that mobile commerce is giving them the power to reach out at all touch points.

The Forrester Research Online Retail Forecast from 2013 through 2018 shows that:

- Social media usage is now a part of daily lives of people— people visit social networks almost compulsively. Number of people using social media apps has increased, with people checking these sites while at work and even while in the bathroom.
- The average American household has high definition television (HDTVs) (83 percent), Internet-connected computers (80 percent), and smartphones (65 percent).
- Eighty-four percent of smartphone and tablet owners say they use their devices as second-screens while watching TV at the same time.
- On an average day, roughly one million Americans turn to Twitter to discuss TV.

Companies are leveraging these consumer habits and the surfeit of screens to drive online commerce. They attempt to understand and appeal to a generation growing up on digital devices and offer them value through products and omnichannel experiences. By all accounts, they are succeeding.

The Consumer Landscape

The change in buying habits over the last few decades has led to phenomenal changes in the consumer buying landscape. It is a change that had not been conceived by science fiction books or movies. Carrying their smartphones or other mobile devices, people check prices and shop at all times. Single day delivery is a reality. Drones deliver orders within a few hours in some areas. Customers who will not be home to take delivery can have their orders delivered to lockers located in subways which can be opened by a unique code sent to them by the retailer, and can simply collect their orders while walking through.

Companies and retailers are finding new ways to harness technology. They track customers through mobile devices, directing them to the nearest store in the neighborhood or delivering a discount coupon that they can use for their purchase, luring them into a store when they walk past it. Advertising too is done in a focused way, delivering tailor-made messages on their devices. Consumers scan the codes on products and in advertisements, and quickly connect with the company even while on the move. Restaurants enhance their environment with Wi-Fi access, getting free advertising when people share their location with others. Apparel retailers help people try out new clothes on virtual models and help them select what suits them best. Retailers offer online searches for products if they are not available in-store, promising to deliver them quickly if they are available in their inventory anywhere—store, warehouse, or factory.

This has given rise to *anytime, anywhere retail.*

Reimagining Retail

Digital-savvy consumers connect across all channels and touch points. As a result, consumers are empowered and informed. That is a big shift from the past and companies have to reinvent themselves to meet the needs of such customers. It is time to reimagine and reinvent retail.

Oracle's survey (2011) of digital natives (people born after 1980) from the UK, Germany, and France revealed that the shopping experience of the future has to be connected, individualized, and always available. The results of the survey show that companies have to cater to discerning consumers who love to shop, with differentiated products, pricing, and services. Connected consumers interact with retailers when and how it suits them, and want their experience to be seamless across channels. Retailers must, therefore, optimize their operations for customer experience and operate in a connected full-time environment.

"The Internet has quickly become a very serious shopping alternative to traditional 'brick and mortar' retailers," says the IBM Retail 2020 report. E-commerce sites are able to offer huge selection, customized offers, easy availability, and quick delivery, which appeals to people. The report makes several predictions about e-commerce.

1. *The digital generation*: Young people born into the digital world will grow older and dominate shopping in the coming years.

2. *The hourglass effect*: Consumers trade up and down, so that luxury retailers and those offering value do well. But the middle market is expected to shrink in the United States and in other mature markets, creating an *hourglass* effect. Stores catering to middle class customers have to create fresh value propositions.

3. *Growth in emerging markets*: Since markets in developed countries are saturated, emerging markets like Brazil, China, and India will be the engines of economic growth. Brands have to make use of the great size of these markets.

4. *Excess retail space*: Markets will witness excess retail space in many parts of the world. Online retail is going to cause problems for physical retail space, which has grown faster than retail sales growth.

5. *Integrated retail*: Retail has to reinvent itself to combine the advantages of online with traditional business models, and vice versa.

6. *New ways of shopping*: The mobile phone has become an accessory in shopping. People use it to find the location of physical stores, find the best prices, or locate friends who are in the vicinity, and so on. Companies use location-based services to offer localized and personalized offers. Sales persons will be able to do more than sales and become *solution specialists* by helping customers in solving their exact needs.

7. *The big four players*: A set of four big online players will continue to shape online shopping experiences: Amazon, Google, Facebook, and Apple. Amazon dominates in e-commerce with variety, infrastructure investments in technology, and logistics. Google will continue to guide customers to merchants and product information sites, holding great influence about where consumers buy. It also

offers services like Google Offers and Google Wallet. Facebook has a lot of data about its users and what they *like*. Converting this data to influence purchasing habits of its users will open a gold mine and it can become a sizable force in shaping and controlling future consumer behavior. Apple provides an ecosystem for customers with all online services and stores delivering customer experience.

Indeed, the world of brands and how they are sold has changed, posing challenges to the existing ways of doing business. Director of Commercial Experience at Adidas, Chris Aubrey, and David Judge (2012) of JudgeGill write, "Brands need to optimize the physical store so that it can drive operational efficiencies in terms of product range, capital costs and logistics, as well as deliver a consumer-focused experience that is on-brand and drives consumer preference." Bricks-and-mortar offers retail a significant opportunity—to reimagine the role of the store so that it can rise to the challenges of connected customers. Physical retail channels have to be reinvented by companies so that they deliver on four fronts: experience, service, consumer-focused logistics, and integration.

Integrating the Shopping Experience

As a first step, companies have to discover the drivers of online purchases as also the factors that inhibit them. While consumers like the wide variety and ease of buying, there is also a lurking fear—at least in a segment of the population—of goods not matching up to expectations, security of payments, difficulties in getting after-sales service, or manufacturer's guarantees. These are summed up in Table 2.1.

Digital natives buy online comfortably, but others find it difficult to get over their inborn inhibitions. There is a need to understand all segments. Aljukhadar and Senecal (2011) divide online consumers into three categories which form three global segments:

- *Basic communicators*: Likely to consist of older people; these consumers use the Internet mainly to communicate via e-mail and look for information.

Table 2.1 Factors that encourage or inhibit online purchases

Factors leading to online purchases	Factors inhibiting online purchases
Ease and convenience	Delivery of low-quality products
Better prices, quick deliveries; availability	Difficulty in returning products
Huge choice and variety	Difficulty in obtaining after-sales service—call centers are unresponsive
Privacy	Difficulty in getting manufacturer's warranties
Avoiding aggressive salesmen in physical stores	Security issues in payments, risk of misuse of personal data, stealing of data by hackers
Better information and payment terms, deals, and discounts	Difficulty in returns and obtaining refunds
Ability to source products globally	Lack of ability to see and touch products

- *Lurking shoppers*: Consumers who employ the Internet to navigate and shop. Mostly this group consists of highly educated males or females.
- *Social thrivers*: People who use the Internet to interact with each other socially by means of chatting, blogging, video streaming, and downloading. Such people are most likely to be less than 35 years old and fall in the lowest income bracket.

Each segment has to be approached differently. Companies have to make efforts to help overcome the fears of the basic communicators. For lurking shoppers, they have to improve customer experience leading to branding and loyalty. For social thrivers, companies have to improve engagement through relevant messages and content, which leads them to brands.

Sorce, Perotti, and Widrick (2005) studied the buying behavior of younger and older online shoppers and their attitudes toward Internet shopping. They found that while older online shoppers search for significantly fewer products than their younger counterparts, they actually purchase as much as younger consumers. So, though older consumers were less likely to search for a product online, once they had done so, they were more likely to buy it online than younger shoppers. Most shoppers have four objectives for online shopping: convenience, information access, selection, and ability to control the shopping experience.

The key to online customers remains enhancement of customer experience using the above four elements. Integrated across channels, it leads companies to omnichannel retail.

Exhibit 2.1

Integrating Physical and Virtual Worlds: General Electric's Direct Connect Program

The *Always-On* customer requires companies to integrate all channels. Distribution channels must merge with sales, service, and information channels to provide real-time information to customers. Companies understand this and integrate the information available online with their capabilities in physical supply chains for wide-ranging savings. This exhibit shows how General Electric (GE) was able to reduce costs through integrating channels in its white goods division.

Treacy and Wiersema (1995) describe how the company was able to integrate online channels to help reduce inventories and thereby heavy investments in distributing products. Traditionally, the business operated on the principle *a loaded dealer is a loyal dealer*, that is, if dealers have excess stock, they would be committed to sell it and would not be able to stock goods of anyone else.

However, this thinking was becoming irrelevant as retailing changed. Low-cost retailers gained a distinct advantage over GE dealers. In the 1980s, therefore, GE decided to transform itself and become a *low-cost, no-hassle supplier to dealers*. It abandoned the loaded dealer concept and decided to build operational efficiency instead. Dealers were connected to the company's supply chains and depended on *virtual inventory*—a computer-based inventory system—and no longer had to stock excess stocks and incur carrying costs.

GE's Direct Connect program helped link dealers to the company's own inventory. Dealers were now able to access hundreds of models and show them as lying in their warehouses, though they did not have them. Customers could see and experience the few models that were available in stores and see the variations on computer terminals. The model selected by the customer is ordered on Direct Connect and immediately shipped by the company from the nearest warehouse.

In this way, the company reduced inventories across channels and integrated dealers into its own system. In turn, dealer information, such as customer data and movement of goods, was made available to the company in real time. The company saved distribution costs through the system, while the dealer operations also became more efficient. By linking the system to order processing and demand forecasting and production, the company operates to consumer demand rather than loading dealers. The company backed up the system by creating 10 warehouses that can deliver 90 percent of the orders in 24 hours.

The experience of GE's Direct Connect program shows that companies can gain by:

1. End-to-end integration of supply chains;
2. Standardizing operations and systems; and
3. Management systems that favor integrated and high-speed transactions.

Omnichannel Retail

Omnichannel retail has become a reality because people move across channels seamlessly. In omnichannel retail, all channels, including online and offline ones, track and entice customers. This is necessary because consumers do not distinguish between online and offline channels. A consumer will, for instance, see a hoarding and his mind will connect it with the store display or TV commercial, and in turn with previous experiences and store ambience seen earlier.

Integration of channels is, therefore, an evolutionary response to the changed environment. Physical stores face a threat from e-commerce, so they must use online channels to offer a seamless experience. Online companies, on the other hand, find that they must deliver a physical experience so as to deliver customer experience at all touch points.

That is why companies must combine their online and offline experiences. They must first connect various channels, and then go beyond connecting those channels, converging them with customer touch points. Though companies treat these activities as different departments, customers view them as one company, whether online, in-store, on a mobile device, tablet, or anything else. They want a multichannel experience with seamless interactions, with a availability. This gives rise to the opportunity to offer personalized promotions and interactions so as to engage the consumer.

To meet the expectations of the customer, companies exploit technology to expedite the shopping experience, optimize their operations, and develop multichannel strategies. Brick-and-mortar stores remain critical in the shopping experience of the future. Physical stores exhibit products and deliver great shopping experiences, while online services allow customers to explore the complete range, compare prices, and learn from others.

Physical retail channels have to deliver on four fronts: experience, service, consumer-focused logistics, and integration into omnichannel systems. Aubrey and Judge (2012) mention that the omnichannel approach is the *new normal*—companies have to adapt to a commercial landscape in which value-oriented and omnichannel consumers are in control. They have to absorb the higher costs related to the extending supply chains across channels.

Online retailers try to deliver a good offline experience, while brick-and-mortar retailers increase their reach through online offerings. Growth comes from two developments. First, as the use of smartphones and tablets spreads, consumers are spending more time online to explore products. Second, traditional retailers are increasing their online involvement.

Thus, *omnichannel* actually is a survival strategy: Threatened by the online onslaught, traditional retailers are left with no option but to follow their customers on the Internet. For example, the leading bricks-and-mortar chain, Macy's, tracks customers by installing 24 tracking cookies on a visitor's browser, according to *MIT Technology Review* (Regalado 2013). It combines other channels well: It uses TV advertising with a celebrity, Justin Bieber, who asks customers to download its mobile app, which

Table 2.2 Integration strategies used by online and offline merchants

Company category	Integration strategy
Online merchants	Improve delivery systems Offline experiences and customer service Physical stores for display, trials, *click and pick* and *click and collect*
Offline stores	Provide detailed information about products online Salespersons help in-store search using tablets Take orders online and deliver from stores Real-time inventory tracking across stores Interactive boards and screens enabling customer engagement

guides them to stores. During shopping, the app is used by customers to scan the QR codes on products and to connect with the company. The chain of more than 500 Macy's stores are used as distribution centers, from where online orders are shipped.

Companies such as Macy's integrate offerings so as to provide convenience and seamless shopping experience through cross-channel delivery options such as *click and collect* or *click and pick* services. Retailers and consumers interact with each other online through mobiles, tablets, and kiosks, while in physical stores.

How companies are integrating channels to deliver a seamless customer experience is summarized in Table 2.2.

This phenomenon is not limited to the rich countries only. Across the world, people are using smartphones to research purchases, find stores, look for best prices, and make payments. It has emerged as an instrument of empowering people in poor countries, who can now spend and receive micro payments and conduct transactions through their mobile phones.

Developing Countries: Leapfrogging to a Connected World

While consumers in developed economies see integration of channels and improved customer service through integration of channels, e-commerce is being ushered in by mobile phones through entirely different and unique ways in developing countries, changing the lives of the poor. For instance, *The Economist* reports that the poor are using them in innovative ways to increase their business. *Beeping*, or the practice of hanging up after a single ring, has become a free messaging system: Street hawkers assign special ring tones to different customers and become the means of placing orders.

E-commerce is being helped in such countries by the falling prices of smartphones. The average selling price of Android smartphones was $254 in 2014, and was expected to fall to $215 in 2018. Google launched Android One in 2014, which enables partner companies to sell smartphones for $105. In emerging markets, local manufacturers are able to offer smartphones that are less than $100; price tags of $50 are a reality in many parts of the world.

Perhaps never before has a technology penetrated so fast to the poor. It has given a boost to commerce, enabling even small traders to benefit from technology.

The way that e-commerce and mobile payments work with the poor is entirely different from the Western world, fulfilling a more important role. In the more developed countries, most people have bank accounts and the mobile phone serves as an additional payment channel. In emerging economies, it is being used to empower poor people who do not have bank accounts or access to formal banking. Since many developing countries have nonexistent or poorly developed financial infrastructure, transactions are done mostly in cash. The poor—because they live in remote areas or lack education—mostly remain outside the banking system. Low levels of financial inclusion condemn the poor to make use of informal systems, which have high interest and transaction costs. This poses a barrier for social and economic development.

Mobile money has helped financial inclusion of the poor in emerging countries. A growing number of people in remote areas are now using mobile phones for payments. One such innovation is M-Pesa, a mobile phone-based money payments service developed by Vodafone and launched by its Kenyan affiliate, Safaricom. M-Pesa helps people to make very small electronic payments and to store money using ordinary mobile phones. People use their phones to transfer funds to M-Pesa users and nonusers, pay bills, and purchase mobile airtime credit for a small, flat fee of 2 percent per transaction. The low fee has helped penetration among the poor and enabled them to get access to formal financial services that they lacked.

Mobile money systems such as M-Pesa enable people to use formal banking and financial services, freeing them from money lenders. It allows millions of people to get access to financial services cheaply and securely. In Kenya, for example, active bank accounts increased from 2.5 million in 2007 to more than 15 million in 2011. Unbanked consumers using the mobile banking service M-Pesa doubled between 2007 and 2009. They saved transaction costs of approximately three dollars per transaction; M-Pesa is being used not only for transactions but also for savings. More services are being added as people get access to better technology. These include financial services such as credit, insurance, merchant payments for goods and services purchased, governments payments, and to collect tax revenues.

It is estimated that M-Pesa transactions in Kenya outnumber the total number of worldwide transactions made by Western Union. In many countries, governments are allowing e-money and the operation of non-bank operators. Together with the success of electronic remittances, digital payments are leapfrogging the need for building costly formal banking structures. Similar systems like easypaisa, t-cash, and others have been launched in other countries, with varying degrees of success.

Mobile money helps people in emerging economies to:

- Make money transfers;
- Pay bills for utilities and services;
- Receive government payments such as social security payments, salaries, and pensions;
- Access banking services; and
- Purchase airtime.

Companies eye the market opportunities that technology opens up in emerging countries. They look at the sheer size of markets in Brazil, China, Africa, and India to sell their products. Brands are already entering these countries through online offerings.

More important, many countries are *leapfrogging*—that is, jumping to a new technology without going through intermediary technologies. Mobile phone technology, for instance, is available in many developing countries and areas where even landlines were not available. "By leapfrogging technologies like telephone and cable landlines, emerging markets will be able to access productivity-enhancing technologies for a tiny fraction of the cost," explains (Ernst and Young, n.d).

The E-finance Revolution

E-finance is a revolution for poor countries. Evidence indicates financial inclusion is starting to happen. In many African countries, electronic cash and multipurpose cards help in savings and payments for customers who often do not even have formal bank accounts. Countries like Brazil, Estonia, and the Republic of Korea show that e-finance can be introduced quickly even where basic financial infrastructure is weak.

"The service has brought millions of people into the formal financial system, hobbled crime by substituting cash for pin-secured virtual accounts, and created tens of thousands of jobs," writes Mutiga (2014).

Some developing countries show how leapfrogging has changed lives. In Zimbabwe, Botswana, Cote dŌIvoire, and Rwanda, wireless phone subscribers outnumber fixed-line users. Cambodia has a low per capita income, but the country has a high mobile telephone penetration, according to a report by the World Bank (Claessens, Glaessner, and Klingebiel 2001).

The initial fears of consumers to pay online have been overcome in many countries by higher security standards. People trust the e-commerce sites that take responsibility for payments and refunds. E-commerce payments fall in the category of Card Not Present merchants, since customers do not swipe cards. Multiple verification systems and enhanced security standards have to be used to make online payments safe, and fight a constant battle to remain one step ahead of the hackers.

E-commerce is changing the way business is done. It has many faces: In the developed world, the use of big data defines anticipating and fulfilling customer needs. In emerging economies, it offers people, even those living in remote areas, to buy products and brands that they had no access to earlier. Also, in poor economies, as people get used to using online payment services, markets will leapfrog and mature into full-fledged e-commerce sooner rather than later.

There is little doubt that e-commerce is the future everywhere. How it evolves and how companies make use of opportunities globally remain to be seen. Innovative apps are waiting to be built and technologies continue to evolve and develop to take e-commerce to entirely new directions that we cannot imagine today.

To develop it further, businesses have to look at the characteristics of the connected consumers like Mary, their needs and motivations, and their ease in dealing with omnichannel buying in the next chapter.

CHAPTER 3

The Connected Customer

Mary's life is centered around her mobile and she uses it for so many things: She posts comments and status, quickly checks for reactions from friends, takes pictures and shares them, checks for updates and news, and uses apps that she likes. Can companies understand her and what she wants by identifying moments of truth and increasing engagement? Further, can they customize things to be exactly what Mary wants? If they can do that, Mary will not only be a customer but become a partner with the company—she will give ideas to it about new things to make, becoming a co-creator.

In this chapter, we explore the buying behavior of connected consumers.

Earlier, they went to the store and bought what they needed, guided by knowledge about brands that they had picked up from TV, newspapers, or friends. Now they tap into their connected devices, look for products and reviews, order and pay online, and have the products delivered quickly at home.

Mobile devices have become so convenient that people do many tasks by tapping on them—tasks that earlier required going somewhere and standing in a queue. Indeed, apps are multiplying by the day—more than one million apps are available today for getting things done. People just need to tap the app and pay their bills, book movie or travel tickets, search for friends, and buy products. They take pictures and share quickly with friends. The Internet of Things makes it possible to control devices in the home through a smartphone. As more things are connected by means of automatic sensors, the limits of what people can do with connectivity will be pushed even further.

People are also becoming comfortable with interacting with brands and buying online. A Nielsen report, *How Digital Influences How We Shop around the World* (2012), says that though products like apparel, books, travel, and consumer electronics have the highest digital shopping intentions, food and beverages purchase online has also increased in two years. Customers are now open to buy a variety of things online, including skin care and cosmetics, electronic books, and digital newspaper and magazine subscriptions. While computer games, software, entertainment tickets, and music have traditionally been sold on the Internet, people now look for newer categories of products like groceries, apparel, accessories, shoes, and even jewelry.

For consumer packed goods category, the survey found that shoppers are more likely to adopt an omnichannel approach, where online shopping becomes a supplement to traditional brick-and-mortar retailing. Today, customer experience is enhanced by integrating online and offline channels in a variety of ways, as shown in Table 3.1.

The changed buying behavior is leading to the era of consumer engagement, which in turn is forcing companies to interact through customer-focused channels (Figure 3.1).

Table 3.1 *Consumer experience is enhanced by online channels*

Offline experience	Online experience
Browse through the limited products on display, touch and feel products	Browse through unlimited products, compare prices, get advice
Limited by store timings and distance	Shop for products anytime and have them delivered at a convenient time at home or placed in a locker
Physically try out products that have been researched before; shopping as a social experience	Search products, see videos, check dimensions, view what others have to say. Can try out products on their virtual avatars
Dependent on the salesperson	Let people see and browse products and assist only when necessary
Cannot avail real-time offers, provides limited data to the store	Real-time personalized offers delivered to customers during the shopping process, customer shares huge amounts of data that helps build customer relationship management (CRM).

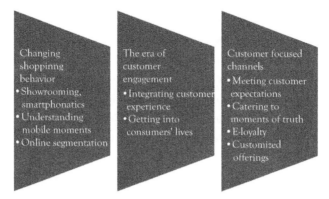

Figure 3.1 The connected consumer is forcing a host of changes across channels

Changing Shopping Behavior

Consumers use the Internet for conducting research about products, search for deals, compare prices, look for promotions and coupons, provide feedback through social media, and use a digital shopping list.

Indeed, the way that people look for products and search has gone through a tectonic shift. Also, it goes beyond merely searching for information. Two trends that are clearly visible in consumer behavior are showrooming and smartphonatics.

- *Showrooming*: The phenomenon where consumers visit brick-and-mortar stores to check out products on display, but then buy them online after surfing for the best deal. They look at the gadgets, see trials and demonstrations, check the best prices offered—and then walk out. This is seen as a real threat to physical stores that invest in infrastructure and provide a pleasing ambience, only to find customers ordering online. Very often shoppers use their smartphones to check online prices even as they are shopping in stores, checking out products physically. The popularity of online stores was seen as a death knell for brick-and-mortar stores. But retailers have fought back: A report by *Business Insider* (Adler 2014) says that *reverse showrooming* or *webrooming* is also happening, which is when consumers search online, but then head to a bricks-and-mortar store to buy the products. Helping these trends are techniques like employing knowledgeable sales staff, integration of online and offline orders, in-store Wi-Fi, smartphone discounts, and making shopping a social experience.

- *Smartphonatics*: Consumers who change their shopping, banking, and payment behavior after switching to a smartphone form a new category known as the *smartphonatic*. *Time* (Kadlec 2012) reports that globally, a quarter of smartphone owners are considered smartphonatics, consisting of people who use their phones for mobile banking and mobile payments. They use their devices to check out prices and order even as they are on the move. Such consumers photograph objects and bar codes as they go about doing other things, and check out products, seek opinions, check out prices and deals, and order online.

These two trends show that channels are getting integrated, where consumers switch from one mode of engagement to another seamlessly. It also shows the importance of mobiles in the lives of people. Increasingly, life is becoming a collection of mobile moments.

Understanding Mobile Moments

Life has become a collection of mobile moments for many people. "Our lives have become a collection of mobile moments in which we pull out a mobile device to get something done immediately wherever we are," writes Schadler, Bernoff, and Ask (2014) of Forrester Research, in their book, *The Mobile Mind Shift*.

Can companies get into these mobile moments of their customers? Can they get them talking about brands even while they are doing all those smart things on their phones? The first step to answer these questions is to understand the online behavior of consumers.

An AOL and BBDO study *Seven Shades of Mobile* (2012) shows how people use mobiles. It found that 68 percent of consumers' smartphone use occurs at home. The most common activity is not shopping or socializing, but engaging in *me time*. Apart from games and music, *me time* is also used to check websites and apps: checking out the latest tech gadgets just for fun, viewing the weather in other places because it is entertaining, ordering pizza, checking out on gossip or what others are doing, and so on.

Brands and companies try to get into this *me time* and the activities that consumers are doing online at that time without being intrusive. This can only happen if the brand messages and content are relevant to consumers in order to engage them.

The study found seven ways that consumers are active on their phones for the following activities:

- *Accomplish* (11 percent)—Managing finances, health and productivity, activities, and lifestyle;
- *Socialize* (19 percent)—Interacting with other people;
- *Prepare* (7 percent)—Planning for activities including travel, movies, attending events, and so on;
- *Me time* (46 percent)—Relaxation and entertainment, or to simply pass the time. Includes watching videos, following news and gossip, playing games, and window shopping;
- *Discover* (4 percent)—Seeking news and information;
- *Shop* (12 percent)—Finding and purchasing a product or service; and
- *Self-express* (2 percent)—Participating in hobbies and interests.

Despite *me time* being the biggest usage of phones, it was found that brands do not perform well in this category. This is because consumers saw the ads placed in *me time* as irrelevant and got in their way, as they were interested in other things. If, for instance, one opens a video and an ad starts playing, it is a matter of irritation and does nothing for the brand. Clearly, brand messaging has to align with what people are doing at that time, so that it does not interrupt, but enable messaging that entertains, makes people laugh, and is relevant to their interests.

That can happen only when companies know which segments they are dealing with.

Online Consumer Segmentation

By studying their usage patterns with mobile devices and apps while researching and purchasing products, Vivaldi Partners (2014) has identified five distinct segments of *Always-On* consumers. They include *mindful explorers* (27 percent), *social bumblebees* (22 percent), *ad blockers* (20 percent), *focused problem solvers* (18 percent), and *deal hunters* (13 percent). These segments have the following characteristics:

- *Mindful explorers*: People in this category like to explore information from many sources, and look for reviews and opinions. They buy only what they need. They interact with retailers and are usually early adopters of new products. They can become loyal brand advocates and usually make online purchases about once a month.
- *Social bumblebees*: This category consists of about one-fourth of consumers. The social bumblebee is a spontaneous shopper and likes to share experiences online. Usually a young professional, the bumblebee spends a large part of the day online and makes online purchases regularly.
- *Ad blockers*: Ad blockers are concerned about their privacy and get irritated by intrusions by companies into their personal space. They have a close circle of friends and loved ones with whom they like to go out and shop, and also interact with them through social networking sites. Such people are likely to buy cooking and cleaning supplies and household staples online.
- *Focused problem solvers*: People in this category are likely to be older. They spend less time online than the previous categories. Their online shopping consists of staple household and personal care products. Such people like to see and experience products and are likely to buy bigger purchases

Table 3.2 Targeting online segments

Segment	Percentage of population	Marketing approach
Mindful explorers	27%	Offer opportunities to engage and explore; compelling content to entice them
Social bumblebees	22%	Opportunities to experience and share; involve friends and family
Ad blockers	20%	Track through big data analysis; provide targeted offers based on needs
Focused problem solvers	18%	Optimize search engines; track through mobiles and send offers when they are shopping
Deal hunters	13%	Offer deals and discounts, bundled offers, horizontal tie-up with partners

from physical stores though they may obtain information online.

- *Deal hunters*: Usually consisting of young couples with growing children, deal hunters like to browse websites and stores, spend time gathering information, and look for the best deals. Discounts attract them. Though people in this segment may visit websites of brands and companies, they are not much engaged with brands and branded content.

An understanding of how people use their connected devices and their behavioral mindsets help us to create strategies to engage them with brands. How the above segments can be targeted is summarized in Table 3.2. The next step is to integrate consumer experience.

Integrating Customer Experience

Customers engage with brands in a variety of ways. Schmitt (2012) describes three layers of consumer engagement—object-centered, self-centered, and social—going from inner to outer layers. In the initial stage, customers' attention is on the object, in which they assess functionality and the benefits expected from it. They acquire information and compare it with other products. At the second level, consumers see how the brand fits in their lives and its personal relevance. At this stage, the consumers identify the product or brand with themselves. At the third level of engagement, consumers view the brand from an interpersonal and sociocultural perspective. They assess how they can acquire social status through the brands or develop a sense of community.

A girl buying a dress, for example, views it first from its quality and looks, second, how it would look on her, and third, whether she gets compliments from friends when she wears it. All three things happen simultaneously in her mind: Consumers subconsciously integrate the three levels of engagement and combine all the information they obtain. The consumer does not see the object and its experience as distinct but as one delivered across different platforms and touch points. That is why all platforms must be presented as one experience.

We have seen in Chapter 1 that the consumers interact with brands not only through media and stores, but also with multiple channels during their purchase journey. This is illustrated in Figure 3.2. Right from need recognition to information search and evaluation, there is continuous interaction with physical stores, traditional media, online search, as well as interaction with social groups.

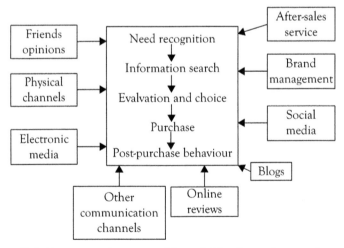

Figure 3.2 Consumers interact with multiple channels at each stage of the purchase decision

As apps and technologies improve, the interaction is becoming gradually more seamless. Customers move back and forth between channels with ease. Any interaction at any stage can become a trigger for purchase. All the channels become the means to explore and interact with companies. The purchase process proceeds in the following ways:

- *Need recognition*: What customers do online gives insight into customer needs. As they search or browse sites, or post comments or seek advice, they leave behind a trail of data that companies can tap to find out about their needs. Many companies go a step further—they learn to anticipate future customer needs by following this data trail.
- *Information search*: This stage is helped by cookies, which track the visitor's browsing. Information search can then be influenced by targeting advertisements or solving customer problems in other creative ways.
- *Evaluation and choice*: Apps help in product evaluation by easy comparisons, updates, and better communication, or by guiding customers to the store.
- *Purchase and postpurchase*: Crucial stages when consumer can influence others by WOM and they cannot be ignored as they were in traditional marketing. This is also the stage when relationships are strengthened through better CRM methods.

Consumers do not regard online experiences different from offline ones. Whether online or offline, it is the same company behind the experience. Gulati and Garino (2000) write that the distinction between dot-com and physical stores is rapidly fading. Since customers do not distinguish between offline brands and online purchases, companies are learning that *success in the new economy will go to those who can execute clicks-and-mortar strategies that bridge the physical and the virtual worlds.*

This can be done in several ways. Retail stores offer *augmented products* which are a combination of product attributes and benefits—and this can be done easily online by the consumer. People are able to combine whatever product attributes they seek and order accordingly.

Fashion sites, for example, offer combinations of clothes and accessories that consumers can mix, match, and order. Such sites are trying to combine offline experiences with their online trade to enhance the shopping experience.

But the integration must go further. In the era when customers were not connected, companies separated marketing activities into different departments of advertising, sales, service, and so on. These departments were managed like tight silos, with each having their own managers who had very little to do with each other. Many back office marketing functions were outsourced, which were done by contractors who had no idea what the rest of the company was doing. This was quite weird: For example, customers were sold products by sales people who painted a very rosy picture, but if something went wrong, they could not get through the company helplines while the sales persons were chasing other leads. Getting through to after-sales service department was next to impossible, as people could not get past the automated voice systems or if they did, the agents could not solve their problems. Instead of providing better after-sales service, all that the customer service departments delivered was anger against the brands.

Today's consumers will have none of this. A bad experience with any department is a failure of the company and consumers do not hesitate to be vocal about it. Now they have the power and freedom to write about their experiences and broadcast them. Bad experiences are not forgiven, and comments are written immediately on review sites and shared with friends. Sometimes these messages go viral, causing immense harm to brands. As a consequence, companies have to manage customer engagement at all touch points, across different channels, quickly and in real time. A report by McKinsey (2012) says, "Companies will be better off if they stop viewing customer engagement as a series of discrete interactions and instead think about it as customers do: a set of related interactions that, added together, make up the customer experience."

Customer experience in today's era is not a series of departmental activities because people are not interested which department they are dealing with. They see their interactions—including the product, the in-store experience, service, telephone, and online experience as *one* experience delivered by the same company. A bad experience at any touch point will result in denting the confidence of the customer. That is why it becomes extremely important to manage each moment of truth—the point in time when the consumer comes in contact with a company message or service—in one integrated manner.

Managing Moments of Truth

Moments of truth (MOTs) occur when a person comes in contact with a brand or message. They happen when one sees an advertisement on television, comes across a brand message online, sees a hoarding on the way to work, or comes across the brand at store displays, promotions, or someone else using that brand.

Connected consumers search online for the products they need before making purchase decisions. They look for recommendations and reviews online. Such behavior has given birth to new MOTs, which were ignored by traditional decision-making models such as AIDA and the funnel model.

MOTs are divided into four successive stages of engagement.

- *Zero moment of truth (ZMOT)*: Google (Lecinski 2011) defined ZMOT as the moment when the consumer searches for something online. In the connected world, this is fast becoming the first exposure to a product or brand. Moran, Muzellec, and Nolan (2014) describe this as *consumer-led information cycle*.
- *First moment of truth (FMOT)*: The FMOT, coined by Procter & Gamble in 2005, describes the actual purchase of the product or the brand.
- *Second moment of truth (SMOT)*: Experiencing or using the product is described as the *SMOT*.
- *Third moment of truth (TMOT)*: The TMOT occurs when consumers share their experiences with the brand.

The MOTs can be summarized as: *stimulus, shelf, experience.*

The MOTs become loops for other customers, building a cycle where new customers continue to get added. For instance, a person's TMOT will become ZMOT for another person. This may happen online, when people read the experience that has been shared on a social network, or offline, when friends see the person using the product.

The implications of analyzing MOTs and consumer behavior are:

1. *Messages are now conversations*: Consumers do not rely on advertising messages alone; one-way communication is now a thing of the past. Today they engage with brands and take part in conversations online. What they share and say about products is voluntary and independent, but more important as it has the power to influence many others.

2. *Importance of WOM has grown*: The earlier WOM was limited in reach and was soon forgotten. Now WOM has the potential to reach millions and is saved digitally for anyone to access and read.

3. *Each MOT is important*: Companies cannot ignore any MOT or consumer experience—each can grow disproportionately on the Internet. Further, consumers even look for small details on the Internet and are quick to post their experiences online.

4. *MOTs are converging*: With increasing usage of smartphones and better technologies for online payments, the stimulus, shelf, and experience stages are delivered by connected devices, making all the MOTs converge.

The important thing to note here is that each MOT can result in positive or negative experiences, which in turn has the potential create WOM publicity and thus the potential to influence other consumers.

Managing WOM Interactions

WOM spreads fast online. Reviews and comments on blog posts, Twitter, and social networking sites spread quickly. Companies hope people, their friends, and friends of friends will help spread positive experiences across the billions of users of social media, convincing some of them, at least, to buy the brands.

A report by Google and Ad Age (2014), *Brand Engagement in the Participation Age*, reveals that 90.8 percent of respondents regularly engage with brands online. Among these, 62.8 percent are hyper-engagers, who engage with companies once per week or more. Another 28 percent are engagers, who engage with brands moderately with a frequency of less than once per week. About 9.3 percent people, called traditionalists, do not seek engagement with brands online. This means that companies have an opportunity to engage and involve a majority of connected consumers. The report lists down core engagement insights about consumers as follows:

1. *Engaged customers buy more*: The *Always-On*, device-carrying consumers of today, dubbed as Generation C, are active consumers. They are a psychographic group with shared values and shared interests in creating and sharing. The report shows that people in Generation C have high propensities to buy. Those who engage more correlate with those who purchase more: It was found that hyper-engagers are more than four times more likely to purchase a product online than engagers.

2. *Consumers want to be inspired and engaged*: Companies have the opportunity to inspire consumers and convert them into dedicated fans by matching their advertising with consumer interests across channels. People, for example, love to watch videos online, as can be seen from the success of YouTube. TV, websites, online video, and banner ads can be integrated to get maximum mileage for brands. People can be encouraged to become influencers to build WOM and social media recommendations. This is a powerful tool because people—even the traditionalists—get influenced by others and look for online recommendations.

To manage the MOTs and WOM communications, companies have to get into the lives of their customers, understand them, and be relevant to them.

Getting Into Customers' Lives

For years, companies have tried to understand consumer behavior. Using market research, they tried to get into the lives of their customers and figure out how they would respond to marketing stimuli. In the connected era, consumers willingly share their personal data and their thoughts and ideas. They also unwittingly leave data trails as they browse websites, which companies can analyze to know what goes on in their minds.

Seybold (2001) writes that companies must understand *customer scenarios*, or the *broad context in which a customer does business*. That is, they must try and find out the context in which customers select, buy, and use products and services. Companies have collected and analyzed data on consumers and products, but have missed out on the big picture of how products and services fit into the real lives of their customers and how they solve problems. Steve Blank (2014) writes further that companies must develop a deep understanding of the buyer, which includes finding out the need that the products fulfill, the time they spend using them, and how their life would change after they have the product.

The question that companies face today is, *how do we get into the lives of connected consumers without being intrusive?* Sending unwanted messages or at the wrong time will merely result in customers turning away from the company.

The idea is to dovetail individual motivations with commercial activities, and to do this, companies must operate within the social and cultural contexts of consumers. Many companies have indeed learnt to involve customers by developing the following capabilities:

- *Process large amounts of data*: Mobile devices provide a wealth of data to companies about customers, such as their location, what they may be doing, and even their emotional state. As more sensors come into existence, companies will have the means to get data from many other sources. This data helps companies get inside the lives of their customers and can individualize their offerings to them. The idea is to know customers so well that companies can anticipate their needs well in advance. Information obtained from stores gets integrated with the information received through apps, sensors, and touch points to know what a customer is going to need, and provide that service.

- *Availability across devices*: Rapidly changing technological environment forces change in the devices that people use. Not only do companies have to be on existing devices like tablets, computers, and televisions, but also keep a track of developing technologies like wearable devices, for instance. Companies have to be available on all devices and build partnerships for developing apps with every new device.
- *Provide ease and convenience*: Connected consumers look for ease and convenience, above all else. Companies must have a *customer obsession* so as to respond to customer needs at all times. This has become all the more important because if a service provider is sluggish or not available, other people will build apps and wean away customers.
- *Quick response*: Mobile devices allow customers to quickly connect with anyone, resulting in their increased expectations. Consumers want everything quickly and now! They expect companies to respond quickly too, just as they can. Companies have to become agile and must build systems and infrastructure to respond quickly to customer concerns. The bureaucratic functioning of marketing departments is now a thing of the past.

Along with the culture of focusing on customers, companies must orient all channels to be focused on the consumer, as the next section shows.

Consumer-Focused Channels

All company channels, which include physical stores, websites, kiosks, direct mail and catalogs, call centers, social media, mobile devices, television, networked appliances, and so on have to be customer focused. There is no back office and no front office, but just one integrated experience across all these channels.

Rigby (2011) writes that soon it will be hard even to define e-commerce, let alone measure it. Consider the modern shopper who can do any of the following:

- A customer goes to a store and likes a dress, but the exact size is not available. The retailer immediately checks the stocks at all its stores and offers to have the dress delivered from a distant store where that size is available.
- A customer checks in an online store by scanning the QR codes on the phone. A dress is selected and added to a *wish list*. The choice is tweeted to friends and opinions sought from them. After much deliberation, the customer goes to a store with friends, tries it on, and buys it.
- A customer likes a dress and posts a positive review online, which is shared on Facebook. The retailer quickly sends a discount coupon to be used at the next purchase at the store.

The above examples show the effect of the Internet on traditional buying. Whereas online stores provide *click and collect* facilities by offering services physically, traditional retailers are following customers on the Internet, integrating communication channels as well (see Exhibit 3.1).

All this attention has raised the bar of what customers expect from companies. This is discussed in the next section.

Exhibit 3.1

Macy's: Combining Online and Offline Experience

In a sign of the times, Macy's, which has stores across the United States, calls itself as *one of the nation's premier omnichannel retailers* in its Annual Report (2013). The chain offers an integrated consumer experience online and offline: It says its DNA includes events such as the Macy's Thanksgiving Day Parade, Fourth of July Fireworks, flower shows, fashion events, celebrity appearances, cooking demonstrations, holiday traditions, and animated window displays. "We engage customers in stores, online and via mobile devices by offering special experiences, as well as advice and options that bring fashion ideas to life," says its Annual Report.

Consumer Expectations

Being the focus of companies, consumers are becoming a spoiled lot. They have become the *now* generation—people who want instant gratification. Nielsen and NM Incite's U.S. Digital Consumer Report (2012) calls them *Generation C*, consisting of 18–34 year olds' *connected* population. Making up 23 percent of the population, they are the most active online content users. It says, "Their ownership and use of connected devices makes them incredibly unique consumers, representing both a challenge and opportunity for marketers and content providers alike. Generation C is engaging in new ways and there are more touch points for marketers to reach them."

This generation has come to expect a number of benefits, such as:

- *Quick response*: Customers now are not willing to wait for companies to respond to their queries or complaints. Nor will they be pushed from one department to another for service requests.
- *Freebies and discounts*: When websites offer freebies and discounts to acquire new customers, it raises expectations. Consumers begin looking for deals and offers from e-commerce sites.
- *Product returns*: Consumers have come to expect a high level of service from companies. They expect easy product returns and refunds, and secure transactions.
- *Free shipping*: Shipping costs increase the cost of goods and consumers expect free shipping and quick delivery of their online orders. Sites like Amazon offer free shipping to their customers who pay to join a loyalty program.
- *Low prices*: Consumers have the ability to search any website for low prices; so, websites have to make their customers loyal to them.

Once the company succeeds in engaging customers and meets their expectations, it will be rewarded by the loyalty of its customers.

Even though people can switch to a competitor at the click of a mouse, consumers tend to be e-loyal, and loyalty can be cultivated and sustained.

E-loyalty

One would expect that online consumers have less loyalty, since they can easily go to a competitor's site. Yet, Reichheld and Schefter (2000) write that most online customers exhibit a clear proclivity toward loyalty. They write, "Contrary to the common view that web customers are fickle by nature and will flock to the next new idea, the Web is actually a very sticky space in both the business-to-consumer and the business-to-business spheres."

Customers begin to trust certain e-commerce sites and stick to them even though lower prices may be listed on other sites. The evidence indicates that web customers tend to consolidate their purchases with one primary supplier, to the extent that purchasing from a supplier's site becomes part of their daily routine.

The single most important benefit that online customers seek is convenience. They want to do business with a site that makes their lives easier, and they are willing to pay more for that convenience. They find that returning to a familiar site is much more convenient than scouting out a new one.

Strauss and Frost (2012) describe the ways of attracting and keeping customers online. These are:

- *Reputation*: Online reputation is built by being honest, making authentic claims, and follow through on brand promises. It is eroded by intrusive advertising or irritating repeat messages.
- *Relevance*: Information provided online has to be relevant to consumers, since people do not like to be interrupted. Unwanted e-mails are directed to spam folders, telemarketing calls are not answered, and SMS messages are blocked. Technology gives companies the ability to target the most relevant information to their customers.

- *Engagement*: Brand communication is done by engaging customers through content that they find relevant, useful, or entertaining. Consumers can thus build personal associations with brands by uploading their pictures and sharing them with friends.
- *Environmental factors*: Culture, social influence, peer influence, and mass media play an important role in affecting online consumer purchasing decisions. Many companies, for instance, try to create an offline buzz through peer influence or use the mass media and extend it to their online activities.

The new technologies give rise to another opportunity—converting customers into coproducers.

Starting with offering customized products for individuals, companies can take engagement to the next level and involve them for generating ideas, product testing, and test marketing.

Turning Consumers to Producers

Three-D printing allows product customization. Already companies are involving their customers to design their own products, which are manufactured according to individual taste and delivered. A report by Bain and Co (Spaulding and Perry 2013) shows the value of customization. Customers can create their own shirts and handbags to consumer-packaged goods. Retailers use data analysis to present a personalized set of products to their customers. Now brands are taking personalization a big step forward into mass customization. This helps in earning customer loyalty and engagement, leading to better WOM publicity. The study estimates that if 25 percent of online sales of footwear were customized, it would result in a market of $2 billion per year—customers who had availed of customized products tend to engage more with the company.

Customers who designed their own shoes and got what they wanted visited its website more frequently, stayed on the page longer and were more loyal to the brand, leading to higher sales, referrals, and lifetime customer value. By automating customization using the Web, companies can more easily take a customer segment down to the size of one. In five years, this will come to be expected by consumers.

Through mass customization, consumers can customize products automatically and still pay the lowest prices. The simplest example is the way in which people can customize their travel plans by searching for information themselves and choose modes of travel or hotels based on their personal choices. But other products too will be customized in the future and 3-D printing will push the trend toward individual and custom-made offers for the generation of connected customers.

Quirky is an example of involving consumers in manufacturing. It crowdsources innovation and product design by means of a competition for product ideas. If enough people like it, an idea is shortlisted for further refinement. Through the website, people suggest different features, designs, and even the product names and marketing slogans. Then a prototype is made, which is reviewed online and then manufactured at a small factory which has 3-D printers and other equipment. "This prototyping shop is central to Quirky's business of turning other people's ideas into products," writes *The Economist* (2012).

The company then ties up with manufacturers and the product is sold on the Quirky website. People earn *influence points* which can lead to a share in earnings. "You play a role in every single decision we make. Help us decide something as simple as what color we should make a product, or as complicated as how to solve an engineering issue," says the Quirky website.

Similar models will be followed by other companies too. Indeed, companies have to change themselves to remain relevant with hyper-connected consumers. The next chapter describes the changes that are taking place in business models and organizations.

CHAPTER 4

The Connected Company

Mary would smile if she knew that she—and her generation—was forcing companies to redefine marketing and reinvent their business models. Learning from consumer habits, companies are integrating channels and have to get rid of the back-office mentality. Every single system has to be focused on the customer. Even organizational cultures are changing.

If consumers are changing, can companies continue to do business as usual?

Today's consumers pose a great threat to traditional companies, or at least those who do not change with the times. Slowly, as companies evolve and find new ways to engage customers, they too must become connected companies. This chapter finds how companies are changing due to a tidal wave of changed consumer behavior.

Berman (2012) writes that businesses in every industry are under intense pressure to rethink their customer value propositions and operations. They have to rethink the very basis of their business, including:

- Reshaping customer value propositions;
- Remodeling business operations to deliver new customer value propositions;
- Transparency in operations and involving customers; and
- Rebuilding the business model, leading to broad industry transformation.

This means that companies have to reshape the very ways that they do business (Table 4.1). At the heart of this transformation are two main factors: control and transparency. Companies have to learn to operate in an environment in which they no longer control brands and information. Business strategy has long depended on stimuli–response based paradigm

Table 4.1 Paradigm shift in business philosophy

From products to solutions	Brand managers do not own their brands; customers do. Brand loyalty is getting discounted as consumers have access to almost infinite choices online
From promotion to education	Companies do not control their use of marketing communications; Customers choose the communications they want to see Companies use individualized, targeted communications.
From place to access	Companies must integrate omnichannels for business operations; share information with trade partners and customers
From price to value	Transparency in pricing in an era of free-flowing and perfect information

in which companies provided stimuli and waited for something to happen. Now this no longer works as the stimulus is out of their control. So, they have to learn to share more information with their trade partners and customers—if customers are living in glass bowls, so are they.

In the new environment, technology becomes a mindset and is not just a tool to increase operational efficiency. Companies have to transform their operations using digital technologies for greater customer interaction and collaboration. New capabilities have to be built to survive.

"Even the most successful company cannot buy its way to change by applying a little lipstick and altering its appearance with a website. It must be willing to change more fundamental aspects of its way of life," writes Kanter (2001).

We have identified eight transformations required in companies. They are no longer an option to change, but a necessity for survival. These have to be wide ranging and total, and are summarized in Table 4.2.

Today consumers have more power because of their ability to widely disseminate knowledge. They can, therefore force firms to be more transparent. All these themes of transformation are discussed below.

Table 4.2 Companies have to transform themselves in a number of ways to meet the needs of the modern, digitally connected consumer

Focus area	Transformations required
Product	Smart, connected products; adaptive personalization, mass customization, co-design of products with customers
Customer obsession	All functional areas to be focused on customer experience; breaking down of departmental silos; from push to pull
Omnichannel marketing	Integrating experience across all touch points: mobile, online, and physical, and of every conceivable information channel
Data analytics	Integrating information from all sources and using analytics to track customers and to create best offers for them
Integrated supply chains	Digitizing supply chains and sharing information about inventories with dealers and customers; connected inventories and logistics
People and culture	Train people for transparency and sharing, equip them with tools to serve connected customers, focus on empowering frontline staff
Communications	Amplified WOM machine; transition from push to pull, encouraging conversations, using social networks to engage customers across channels
Organization	Digital marketing organization; from chief marketing officer to chief experience officer

Product Transformation

Products are becoming smart and connected. Even as they work silently at customer locations, embedded sensors transmit data to manufacturers, giving advanced information about malfunctions to them. Products *call home*, giving operational data about machines. This results in better functionality and greater reliability. "The changing nature of products is also disrupting value chains, forcing companies to rethink and retool nearly everything they do internally," explain Michael Porter and James E. Heppelmann (2014).

Smart, connected products are forcing best practices across the value chain. Consequently, companies must build entirely new technology infrastructure, consisting of layers of *technology stacks*, including changes in hardware, software applications, operating systems within the product itself, and communications ability with constant monitoring.

Customer Obsession

Companies have to develop a customer obsession because people choose their own channels and communication. This has been highlighted by Michael Porter (2001). He wrote that consumers will value a combination of online services, personal services, and physical locations over stand-alone web distribution. They will want a choice of channels, delivery options, and ways of dealing with options.

Functional departments working in silos are a thing of the past. Today all employees of a company, whether in the marketing function or not, have to learn to treat customers as people and understand their individual stories. From the point of view of the customer, all departments or employees represent the company and they do not want to be pushed from one department to another to resolve their issues. So, a free flow of information and collaboration is required and the silos have to be eliminated to deliver a consistent brand proposition.

Social media is adding to the integration. Deals on e-commerce sites get shared and retweeted on social media platforms, generating buzz. A host of sites depend on social media fans to post their pictures and comments about brands, thus spreading the message. Brick-and-mortar stores, travel websites, restaurants, and practically every business add their presence on social media. E-commerce sites try to acquire the social *skin* to utilize individual influence networks. Indeed, these platforms are intruding into each others' grounds. E-commerce sites try to collect users by offering incentives for people to add their friends, while social media sites add e-commerce platforms, hoping to get a share of online buying. They look for traction by getting referrals, and want to be shared and tweeted by users.

All this activity affects the purchasing cycle even before the purchase journey begins. Consumers research products and look for referrals and warnings from their connections. Giamanco and Gregoire (2012) explain,

> Social media's greatest potential is at the front end of the sales cycle—during the prospecting, opportunity qualification, and pre-sales-call research that lead up to a face-to-face meeting.

Exhibit 4.1

CNN and Its Flight 370 Coverage

As consumers change, so do companies. They learn to rely on real-time consumer feedback to alter their offerings. A case in point is how CNN modifies its programming by listening to customers across channels in real time.

On March 8, 2014, the Malaysian Airlines Flight 370 from Kuala Lumpur to Beijing disappeared from the radar less than an hour after takeoff. The Boeing 777 had on board 12 crew members and 227 passengers from 14 nations. It was an intriguing mystery that ignited interest across countries: How could a huge plane simply disappear? But as the plane was not found, other news started gaining importance and went off news networks after a few days.

Data from three different analytics systems, as well as overnight TV ratings showed that people had not grown tired of the story. Tracking mobile page views and video views, CNN found that both shot up more than 150 percent. Data analytics showed that the story outperformed other articles in the same spot on CNN's homepage. CNN took a decision to dedicate more resources, attention, and time to the story, leading to better viewership than other news networks. The intense coverage paid off. *The New York Times* (Carter 2014) reported that CNN's ratings soared in that week and over the weekend, rising by almost 100 percent in prime time, and even accomplished the rare feat of beating Fox News for several hours.

CNN's use of data to track consumers online and on TV helped it realize that the story interested a large audience. While other networks moved on to other stories, CNN decided to keep the story on air longer. Though this was criticized by media watchers, the fact remained that consumers were lapping up every detail that was telecast, writes Abbruzzese (2014).

The missing plane made a gripping story for most consumers, writes Sally Kohn (2014) on the CNN website. It was a *real whodunnit unfolding live before our very eyes* which immediately caught the people's attention. It made for real-life detective story, giving birth to several theories about what could have happened.

Data helped the company to know that people were interested to know what had happened to the missing airliner. It shows how companies can modify their offerings by listening to customers. CNN had successfully integrated its channels of getting feedback from customers. Usually newsrooms and websites are treated as separate operations, but CNN had integrated its editorial side with its online presence. This has helped CNN to become a network more focused on customer needs: The news network has transformed itself and no longer shows news all the time, changing its programming to what people like to watch. Programs that interest people and international criminal investigations have been added to its offerings. The company uses embraced data to track what to say, how to say it, and also when to stop a particular story.

This is what all consumer companies are doing: keeping track of consumer requirements. The CNN website says that data now forms nearly every part of CNN's editorial decisions. It tracks consumption patterns across the Web, mobile, social networking sites and video, and on third-party sites to help it take decisions about programming. Several tools are available for marketing companies:

Dataminr: It uses powerful algorithms to sift through tweets to identify real-time news and events, recognizing patterns and determining in an instant which information is real and which is not.

Outbrain: Outbrain offers to help Internet publishers increase web traffic to their websites by presenting them with links to related and other trusted content. It analyzes real-time mobile consumption to provide its insights.

Chartbeat: A real-time data service for websites, social streams, apps

Optimizely: A customer experience optimization software for companies

Moat: It is an ad search engine which makes it easy to find ads that are running for the top brands and sites. Moat Brand Analytics measures consumer attention.

Omniture: An Adobe company, it promises to offer integrated solution for all marketing efforts: analytics, social, media optimization, targeting, web experience management, and cross-channel campaign management.

By integrating data and having a customer obsession, CNN updated its model and repositioned itself with modern consumers, making itself more relevant with them. That is what companies and brands have to do: reinvent themselves in the digital era, in which the consumer can switch brands easily, and look for personalized attention. Consumers will only buy what best suits them.

Omnichannel Experiences

Brands have to enable their consumers to use all channels to engage with them: They must provide a seamless experience across channels, keeping consumer's experience foremost in the era of *everywhere commerce*.

The shopper's experience is becoming complex, and therefore harder to manage, says a report by Kanter Retail (2013). Thus, companies have to start with understanding their customers' needs, and then fit content and experiences into their lives, and invest in technology to meet those needs. Digital functionality has to be treated not as a means of promotion or sales, but as a means to engage, complement, and enhance customer experience.

The distinction between online and offline worlds is fast getting blurred. While online shopping offers variety and ease, people still like to go out and shop. "It's a ritual, it's a fundamental anthropological need and it will never disappear," writes Paul Todd in *The Guardian* (2014). So, while technology drives customization and personalization, the need to get out of the house and go shopping will always remain. This is the reason why commerce will be aided by e-commerce and not be eclipsed by it.

The shopping street will, however, adapt. In the omnichannel age, retailers are using a combination of all technologies to serve customers better. Technologies are combined to deliver customer experience in-store and outside it by anticipating needs and meeting them faster than ever before.

Data Analytics

Data generated by the always connected mobile shopper are used to deliver insights into customer behavior. They are analyzed for smarter decision making and identifying new business opportunities. There are three main data sources: data yielded by mobile networks about usage and location of the user; personal data collected through store visits, on social media and the like; and data collected from automatic sensors. In-store behavior, combined with network usage data, help retailers provide an omnichannel, seamless customer experience. A detailed discussion on data analytics is given in Chapter 5.

Supply Chains

Traditional channels focus on distributors and agents, while multi-channel management is customer focused, write Rangaswamy and van Bruggen (2005). Now each stage of the decision-making process can be influenced by a different channel. Physical, electronic, communication and social media, delivery and sales channels—all are used to influence a person's buying behavior. A CISCO report (2011) titled *Unifying Customer Experience*, says that companies must manage total customer experience across all channels through the following five steps:

1. *Understand customers' channel behavior:* The first steps include knowing how customers search for and buy products, which channels they prefer, and how they react to different channels.

2. *Integrate data across channels*: As customers interact with companies across multiple channels, companies must have the means to aggregate data from them. Ideally, companies should have complete customer data integration or a single view of the customer across channels, writes Kumar (2012).

3. *Use and evaluate multiple channels*: Companies decide whether additional channels actually serve the customer in some way. Marketing dashboards and real-time monitoring of channels are used to evaluate multiple channels.

4. *Allocate resources across channels*: Optimal channel mix is worked out; the proportion of resources across channels and making the channel strategy cost effective are challenges at this stage.

5. *Develop a channel strategy*: A channel strategy requires synergy, generating and using data, maintaining relationships with channel partners, and building superior competitive advantage.

People and Culture

A rethink about organizational culture is required too. Fields (2014) describes four forces that are driving that change, which are as follows:

1. *Social media*: People use social media to comment or react on what interests them. Companies have to interpret these conversations, understand the background, norms, and language used by them, and then inject their messages into them.

2. *The human business movement*: People relate to people, not corporations. How then to get people involved with companies and their brands? In the era of transparency, companies have to learn to communicate in a simple, straightforward manner, hiding no information and without attempting to misguide their customers. In other words, they have to treat their customers as humans and also present a human face to them.

3. *The purpose economy*: Consumers look not only for products and brands, but also to solve their own and society's problems. This is the basis of the sharing economy, in which things like cars, rooms, or bicycles are rented out to people who need them. One step ahead, the sharing economy is helping people to come together to solve

some of society's problems like poverty and literacy. Consumers look for opportunities to work with companies and organizations that bring value to their lives and to the society; so, companies have to inject social meaning in their brands. The purpose economy requires a larger purpose than merely selling products.

4. *Rethinking the organization*: Organizations have to be more open because relationships are based on give-and-take: they let in outside culture while removing all stops to interact with customers. Thus, they share platforms on which products and services are based, modifying them as the customer needs dictate.

Communications

Media habits and brand communications have changed. Chaffey (2009) mentions six ways in which consumption of media has changed and how companies can adapt to these changing patterns.

- *From push to pull*: Unlike mass media, the Web is a pull medium, where consumers decide what they want to see, only when they want to, selecting the information they want to see. As a consequence, companies have less control on their communications, so they have to devise ways to make people engage with them online.

- *From monolog to dialog*: Today companies have dialogs with their customers, in contrast with the one-way communication they had in the past. Dialogs help companies to collect intelligence about customers and refine their products and offers. However, at the same time, companies have to ensure that they are not wasting time by entering into a dialog with people who have no intention to buy. An example is of companies that collect online fans and *likes*, but these often consist of people who have no real interest in the company or its brands.

- *One-to-one communication*: Online communications enable one-to-one communication, reaching particular niches or delivering personalized messages to individual customers.

Every customer is tracked individually and communications are sent at the exact time when a need arises, increasing relevance and acceptability.

- *Many-to-many communications*: When customers interact with each other, it results in many-to-many communications, or C2C conversations. Online auction sites and classified advertising show the power of many-to-many communications. However, one danger is that negative communications tend to get out of hand in such conversations.

- *Lean-forward approach*: Traditionally, companies would spend on mass media and then *lean back* and wait for customers to come. Now customers *lean forward* to get information. However, if they do not find what they are looking for immediately, they quickly move on. Companies have to learn to *lean forward* to meet customer expectations.

- *Integration of media*: Traditional media cannot be ignored, and they become an accomplice to online companies to guide customers to websites or applications. Online-only companies have to use mass media to drive traffic. Companies thus have to try to achieve synergy in the use of media.

Organization Structure

When everything has changed around them, it is only logical to expect that companies too will have to change. Achieving customer obsession implies that marketing must pervade the entire organization: All interactions at all touch points must be responded to quickly.

Traditional marketing operates in silos: marketing, sales, service, and distribution. For instance, marketing is concerned with brands, while sales is assigned to a different department, completely divorced from the others. CRM is yet another separate silo, while physical consumer experience is farmed out to retailers. More often than not, one arm of the organization does not know what the other one is doing. However, the customer is not concerned with how a company is organized, but wants that the claims made by the company are upheld by all departments and every employee operating as one unit. Departments have to merge to present one integrated whole, leading to wide-ranging changes to the marketing organization.

One development is to rebrand the marketing department and its officers. Sklar (2014) writes that the role of traditional chief marketing officer (CMO) is dead. The CMO is now a chief customer officer, chief client officer, or chief experience officer to enable deeper customer engagement. Each MOT has to be managed to deliver one seamless and integrated experience for the customer. Clearly, the whole organization has to get involved, not just the marketing department.

The marketing organization thus sheds its hierarchal structure. A report, *Marketing 2020* (2013) published by Effective Brands, describes the marketing organization of the future as highly integrated, such as hub-and-spoke structures whereby the chief experience officer (the erstwhile CMO) is placed in the middle, and managers for all functions are connected as spokes to the center (Figure 4.1). There are no functional departments or silos. Marketing organizations manage experiences by integrating three functions: *Think* (through analytics), *Feel* (through engagement), and *Do* (through product and content).

Figure 4.1 The marketing organization of the future

A report by Gregg, Maes, and Pickersgill of McKinsey (2014) says the pressure is rising on companies to become receptive and responsive. They must listen for the signals from customers and improve their engagement levels. Advanced analytics help understand customer moods and intent, which are used to create a response system that engages customers across all touch points and channels. Court (2007) writes that the change in marketing is resulting in broadening of the CMO's role. The marketing function is now built on a larger role as the *voice of the customer* across the company as it responds to changes in the marketplace.

Changing Role of the CMO

The new role enhances, but also complicates the CMO function. The focus is now on differentiating the customer experience and building better customer relationships. It requires connecting marketing with the entire organization. Marketing officers will be required to accomplish the following main functions:

1. *Discover data-driven insights*: Technology has to be used by marketing officers to listen to customers, engage them, co-opt them in product development, and drive customer loyalty and advocacy. In that sense, it takes over the task of chief information officers. Thus, CMOs will have to use data to find insights for growth. Future CMOs will be problem solvers with strategic marketing skills, rather than traditional market research capabilities. CMOs will have to be analysts who derive insights that can improve growth and marketing ROI.

2. *Design strategies in a multichannel world*: The CMO must be one who designs customer experience across all touch points and channels. Marketing today has the job of integrating experiences across the consumer's buying journey. Sales, service, and distribution can no longer be seen as separate units, for instance, and information has to flow freely among them; all parts of the organization have to be *glued* together with a single objective, and this is certainly not an easy task.

3. *CRM*: Tracking customers in real time gives a boost to CRM programs. CRM analytics employ online analytical processing and

data mining from mobiles and automatic sensors. New tools can identify sales opportunities by combining diverse data with social media activities. Such tools can find associations, recognize patterns, make predictions, and help in improved customer analysis that helps in product development, promotions, solving the problems of customers, sales leads, and so on. Predictive modeling helps identify future consumer needs and tells how customers will respond in the future. Customer sentiment, retention, and costs can also be monitored in real time.

4. *Marketing*: Sales, service, delivery, and even advertising and promotion cannot be treated as separate activities. Today every promotion can be tracked in real time, which means that immediate corrective action can be taken, but only if it is connected to the marketing operation.

5. *Engagement and content*: Companies have to engage customers whenever and wherever they interact with a company—in a store; on the phone; responding to an e-mail, a blog post, or an online review. This can only happen if marketing pervades the entire organization. As we have mentioned, people do not wish to engage with brands on social networks, so marketing has to get into their customers' lives and create platforms and content to get people involved.

6. *Feedback and quick response*: Social media, review sites, and blogs have to be monitored for both positive and negative feedback. Marketing officers have to be tuned to what people are posting on the net, in real time, like Nestle's Data Acceleration Center described in Chapter 7. Companies can respond to negative buzz quickly and avert serious damage, or support positive feedback wherever it is happening.

Increasingly, brands are being defined in social networks through shared experiences, writes Solis in his book, *The End of Business as Usual* (2012). "It is now the responsibility of the brand to lead experiences toward customer satisfaction, loyalty and profitability," he writes. He also writes, "Connected consumers are open to interaction if they trust the company and believe there's something in it for them."

Challenges in Integration

Integration of channels is certainly not an easy task because managers do not like to give up their area of control. The major barrier to engagement is, therefore, organizational rather than conceptual. Integration calls for data-sharing and open systems, so managers' resistance has to be overcome. In its report, *The Changing Role of the CMO*, Vivaldi Group (Bernhard and Olderog 2014) likens today's marketing as soccer, in which the ball is passed between players who must constantly move and collaborate. "Brands have to be constantly on the go (sans media breaks!) on this new playing field, 'This sports analogy captures the changing landscape of the CMO.'" it says.

Paul Hagen (2011) of Forrester Research reports on data gathered on 155 Chief Customer Officers (CCOs) and explains that most company departments are focused on meeting short-term revenue goals. There is enough data available in departments, but no one understands the customers' perspective.

A look at complaints posted on online review sites shows mishandling of communications by companies. Some of the common complaints posted on such sites include:

- E-mails are not answered.
- Telephone numbers provided by websites do not exist or put the customer in automated loops by interactive voice response (IVR) instead of taking complaints.
- Customers do not know how and where the defective goods are to be sent.
- After-sales service was unsatisfactory.
- Companies are not following warranties and guarantees.

Such problems show that companies are not able to achieve integration across channels because different departments do not play as a team. The reasons why companies are not able to do this are as follows:

1. *Leadership*: Companies will succeed in omnichannel marketing not simply because they have more or better data, but because they

have better leadership teams. Big data does not preclude the need for human insight. The success or failure of integration depends on business leaders who can build great teams.

2. *Talent management*: Big data calls for rare skills in cleaning, organizing, and integrating large data sets. Furthermore, these data scientists should also be well versed in the language of business. Such a combination is rare—either there are data experts or good businessmen. Thus, the importance of talent management and retaining teams becomes extremely important in modern organizations.

3. *Technology*: Technology remains a constantly shifting target. New apps and practices makes today's technology outdated as new ones are developed all the time. Companies have to keep abreast of all new developments and harness all new devices and apps to make them a part of their big data strategy.

4. *Decision making*: Data and problem solvers have to be brought together so that the technology is geared toward making business more efficient.

5. *Back-office mentality*: Customer interaction is usually divided into two distinct areas: the front office and the back office, without integration of the two. The back office is usually farmed out to contractors who have no stake in serving consumers. The sooner this mentality is got rid of, the better for the company.

6. *Company culture*: Finally, a huge shift in the company's culture is required, according to McAfee and Brynjolfsson (2012). Managers have to move away from hunches and instinct, but develop a culture of data analytics. Many companies use the HiPPO approach, that is, following the advice of the most highly paid person's opinion. Data are used to support decisions the boss has already made using their intuition. Instead, data should drive decisions, not HiPPOs.

Companies that can overcome these problems stand to gain from the big data revolution. Companies that cannot change themselves may find staring at extinction.

Accelerating Change

The sooner that companies realize the integration, the better will they be prepared to meet the expectations of connected customers. Change is accelerating. An IBM report points to several trends that are forcing change, which are as follows:

1. *Accelerating pace of innovation*: Rapid innovation in mobile technology and development of apps is accelerating change. As new forms of retailing evolve, the competitive advantage of traditional retailers will decrease unless they too evolve.
2. *Evolving retailers*: Innovation will result in new retail formats and structures. So, retailers will have to innovate and respond to consumer habits. Traditional retailers will have to reposition themselves, integrating themselves with online developments. Many retailers have indeed succeeded in doing so.
3. *Major shifts in distribution channels*: Customers want complete transparency and information. Thus, brands and companies have to adapt to changes as they happen, integrating their marketing with supply chains and making it all transparent to customers.
4. *Creative destruction*: Creative destruction, which refers to evolution—destruction of older, less-adaptive businesses, making place for more nimble and efficient players—will continue to transform retail. Today's business will have to incorporate mobile platforms, social networks, and automatic sensors to serve customers better. Those who do not make use of these developments will find it difficult to survive.

The next chapter describes the tools available to companies to analyze the huge amount of data being generated. Every move made by consumers is tracked, and data analytics helps realize that objective.

CHAPTER 5

Data Mining and Analytics

Mary loves the lines of the song, "Every breath you take. Every move you make ... I'll be watching you. Every single day. Every word you say." Companies may well be singing that song today, as they track Mary every single moment of her life. Using techniques of data analytics, they know more about her than even her parents.

In the movie *Minority Review*, as the hero walks into a clothing store, his eye is scanned by a computer and he is immediately greeted by name. The computer also accesses his purchase history to make suggestions and reminds him of the products that he might need.

This is indeed what shopping is evolving into, thanks to a world in which we leave data in everything that we do online. By analyzing this data, companies know quite a bit about us, including our buying habits. Data mining and analytics gives power to companies to identify us and to make product offers to us, just like in the movie.

True, companies have always looked for data about their customers. They want to know who they are, where they live, and analyze their profiles to precisely meet their needs. But getting data about consumer behavior has not been easy. The traditional method consists of arming researchers with questionnaires and getting them filled through surveys or focus groups. This is not a very accurate or dependable method, since consumers do not like to be questioned about their decisions or give their personal data. Worse, they are often not aware of their own motivations for buying things. Brown (2001) summed up the frustration of getting customer data, "Consumers don't know what they want. They never have. They never will. The wretches don't even know what they *don't* want."

Indeed, Henry Ford's famous remark, "If I had asked my customers what they wanted, they would have said a faster horse," shows that consumers operate from existing mindsets and seldom see things from a more innovative angle.

Companies have looked for better ways to track their customers. Now they have that tool: a data deluge that yields almost everything about a consumer through data mining and analytics.

Data Deluge

Called *big data*, it is a powerful tool to know not only about the consumers but also about their behavior and state of mind. It consists of the huge volumes of data that are being created at various points in the global economy, such as:

1. Transactional data, consisting of transactions made by customers, suppliers, and others every day;
2. Data from a growing number of networked sensors in mobile phones, smart energy meters, automobiles, and industrial machines;
3. Data exhaust, consisting of trails of data that people leave behind as they browse, communicate, buy, or search online;
4. Data generated by cookies on people's computers, which collect and send information about the online activities of people. Computers and social media sites enable companies to collect information about their online activities;
5. Data tracked by cell phone usage and apps on phones, which gives information about consumers' precise habits and locations;
6. Information that consumers willingly share on social media sites, including comments, reviews, pictures, and videos, and *ego broadcasting*;
7. Enterprise Application Data that is available in databases of customer relationship management (CRM), Supply Chain Management, Enterprise Resource Management, or on a company's website;
8. Sensors in public places, video recordings from cameras in banks, railway stations, traffic lights, ATMs, and so on;
9. Information about a person's health and state of mind through wearable devices; and
10. Public databases such as government records, telephone directories, census figures, and the like.

The result is an immense amount of data, streaming in from different sources. "Customers are telling us all about themselves, each day, every day. We now create as much information every 48 hours as we did from the dawn of civilization up to 2003," says Mckinsey in its report, *The Data Driven Life* (2013).

How companies use this enormous resource depends on their vision and capabilities. Big data gives information in real time: Every device, shipment, and consumer is providing data on happenings as they occur. Data analytics *is the process of inspecting, cleaning, transforming, and modeling data with the purpose of discovering patterns and drawing conclusions.* It promises to change the way business is done.

The task is not easy because the data come from varied sources and in differing formats, structured and unstructured. Davenport (2014) explains that companies have to develop abilities to integrate internal transactional data with existing databases, comments on social media, credit and loyalty cards transactions, the sites that people visit, and also with automatic sensors that give information about the context of purchasing. All these data sets will be in different formats and a high level of expertise is needed to clean and integrate them with company databases.

Big data is indeed valuable to companies. Davenport (2006) writes, "They know what products their customers want, but they also know what prices those customers will pay, and how many items each will buy in a lifetime, and what triggers will make people buy more." Companies can today identify their most profitable customers, increase the likelihood that their products will be liked, and increase customer loyalty, all through analytical methods.

Making Use of Data

The data analysis ability is not easily acquired, simply because the quantum of data available is huge. Loveman (2003) dubs it as a *future diamond mine*, where millions of individual transactions are available. Barton and Court (2012) explain three steps as to how companies acquire abilities to make use of this enormous data:

1. *Source data from multiple sources*: Companies need systems to get data from multiple sources and consumer touch points.
2. *Build prediction and optimization models*: The data must be used to build analytics models for predicting and optimizing outcomes.
3. *Change the organization*: Data is not merely a resource in modern organizations, but a transformational agent. Traditional marketing structures have to change, as discussed in Chapter 4.

Data analysis involves detective work, by uncovering insights from the streaming data. The detective follows the data trails left by people as they do things.

Consumers' Data Trails

Davenport (2013) writes that powerful data capabilities will apply *not just to a company's operations but also to its offerings—to embed data smartness into the products and services customers buy*. Data analytics and optimization can be built into every business decision, leading to better customer engagement and, consequently, to higher profits. McKinsey estimates that *a retailer using big data to the full has the potential to increase its operating margin by more than 60 percent*. How Apple, Google, and eBay use data trails is illustrated in Exhibit 5.1.

Exhibit 5.1

Getting Personal with Data Mining

Companies are already using data mining techniques to offer personalized products and messages pinpointed to customers. This exhibit shows how three companies—Apple, Google, and eBay—effectively use data to understand consumer behavior.

Apple: Apple's app network connects brands with users where they are most engaged. Its iAd service, which is built into its iOS, helps in precise targeting. Users are analyzed in terms of website preferences, internet usage behavior, apps used, a person's music,

TV and audiobook preferences, devices, demographics, and network. As a result, each ad is shown only to people who will see it, through the apps they like to use. Demographic data and people's unique interests and preferences are used to connect the most relevant brands.

Google: Google collects and analyzes customer data and uses data mining techniques. Its philosophy, as explained on its website, is to *focus on the user and all else will follow*. Information about IP addresses, search terms, and browser types are collected, which helps the company to build a precise profile of people. Data provides Google with information about geographical location with a built-in weather forecast. Through its mail analysis, it provides further insights. Data about music and video preferences are collected via YouTube, and Google Maps gets information on travel destinations and plans.

eBay: The eBay stores more consumer data in its central data warehouse, which is used to get an integrated customer view to generate innovations. In-house departments use the data by building *sand boxes* and compare it with external data.

Data analysts follow trails left by people, picking up details of their habits and purchases. It is like following a fireworks display—the eye knows the light left behind by a bright light as it moves across the sky. Following this data trail in a manner of detectives—dubbed as *digital breadcrumbs* by Alex Pentland (2014)—can give accurate pictures of consumer habits. Data analytics help to link behavioral, transaction, and customer interaction insights into the minds of consumers. Pentland calls this *social physics*—the combination of data reveals how humans interact and how ideas spread. The millions of data points measured over a long period of time in real settings are the *living laboratories* that help us monitor human behavior like never before. For example, Pentland finds how behavior changes when people fall ill; using data from websites and phones, companies can tell that certain people were going to get flu even before they get it. Similarly, advanced analytics help companies to know when purchase decisions are most likely to be made. Some companies have already made strides in this capability (Exhibit 5.2).

Google Analytics helps website owners to know important facts about visitors. Users can set up their own dashboards and track which online campaigns bring the most traffic and conversions, where the visitors are located, and find out what people are searching for and see what they click on. Google Analytics is a virtual powerhouse to understand website traffic and to identify users.

This is not all. Researchers say they can pinpoint personality traits by merely studying user-generated text such as e-mails and social media posts. Eben Haber and his team at IBM has developed software that studies streams of tweets from social media and correlates them to personality, values, and needs. The software can map someone's personality from just about 200 tweets, which helps predict their purchases. Extroverts, for instance, are attracted to advertisements that offer excitement by buying a mobile phone. They also prefer Coca-Cola to Pepsi and Maybelline cosmetics to Max Factor. Pepsi, on the other hand, is preferred by agreeable people.

Exhibit 5.2

Predictive Analytics

Retailers have always collected information on their customers. Target too does that, assigning each shopper a unique code that lets the company track a person's purchase history. The company tracks all interactions—such as using a credit card, filling out a survey, calling the customer helpline, opening an e-mail, or visiting its website—to workout detailed consumer profiles. This data is linked to demographic and geographic information along with bought data about ethnicity, job history, magazines subscribed, banking information, social networking data, and so on to work out detailed product preferences. This information is analyzed and through *predictive analytics* the company can figure out what you want and when. Specific mailers are then sent to customers, and sales of the products advertised skyrocket as a result.

Target could link purchase of certain items like unscented lotion, health supplements, scent-free soap, and extra-big bags of cotton balls to pregnant ladies. The company could also figure out a lady's due date.

New Scientist (Rutkin 2014) reports an algorithm can track flu cases across the United States by mining data. The program is able to predict flu outbreaks in the United States by monitoring what people search for on Wikipedia. The program downloads publicly available information every hour about how many people across the country accessed the pages. By doing so, they could accurately predict the number of cases in the country two weeks earlier and with a difference of just 0.27 percent.

Technologies are being refined all the time to get deeper insights. Whereas earlier, computers could only look at quantitative data, now all kinds of data are analyzed.

The Economist (2014) reports of face-recognition technologies which can extract information about people by tracking the images available online. The Elastic Bunch Graph Matching technique (EBGM), creates a 3D model from two-dimensional images, which can be used to match with any other images. The technology is used to go over video feeds from the growing number of cameras from restaurants, streets, traffic lights, offices, and other sources. "We may not be far from a world in which your movements could be tracked all the time, where a stranger walking down the street can immediately identify exactly who you are," says another report in *The Economist* (2013a).

Another technology is IBM Watson. It helps companies track the natural language that is being posted all the time, as shown in Exhibit 5.3. This represents a giant step toward analyzing the millions of comments that are posted by consumers daily.

Exhibit 5.3

IBM Watson: Big Data Analysis for Marketing

So far, computers have crunched numbers to help in marketing decision making. Managers and researchers must have wondered how nice it would be if a computer could go through the enormous natural language data produced daily—on blogs, Internet conversations on various platforms, Facebook comments, and so on—and produce intelligence about the mood and concerns of consumers. Reading and tracking all this data by humans is impossible, simply because of the size involved. Companies have no way to track what is written on each and every site globally.

IBM Watson does just that. Named after IBM founder Thomas J. Watson, it uses natural language processing and analytics, and processes information just the way people think. This ability represents a major advantage in an organization's ability to analyze and respond to big data. Watson's ability to answer complex questions posed in natural language quickly is a great boon for companies to help assess and predict consumer needs based on what they share on the Internet.

Another advantage of IBM Watson is that users can get insights through visual representations without the need for advanced analytics training, through its natural language interface. The service removes impediments in the data discovery process, enabling business users to quickly and independently uncover new insights in their data. Watson Analytics automatically prepares the data, finds the most important relationships, and presents the results in a visual format for managers.

The ability of Watson to evaluate social media data, publicly available data, and proprietary data from clients and continuously learn from that information is becoming invaluable in many industries. In marketing, a company could train Watson to understand its customers, and then use predictive models to recognize new products or services that their customers will buy. It can analyze and predict consumer sentiment and needs, evaluate new products, or predict which advertising will be effective. For example, it can figure out whether a movie trailer is going to positively affect an audience or not. IBM is now allowing customers to use *Watson as a service* and has opened it up to developers to build Watson apps.

IBM

WATSON
Goes to Work
(For You)

270 BILLION

customer calls are handled annually

Nearly **50 PERCENT**

of all incoming service calls require escalation, dispatch, or go unresolved

61 PERCENT

of customer calls could have been resolved with better access to information

INSURANCE

In the past 12 months, approximately 1 in 6 customers have only interacted via digital channels. This is primarily driven by Gen Y customers, among whom more than 20% of recent interactions are digital only.

Only 44% of health insurance customers and 54% of provider consumers actually tell anyone within a month of having a positive experience, compared to 70% of retail and 66% of banking customers.

Consumers are increasingly looking for personalized, efficient interactions with the companies they frequent. Is your organization making the grade?

FINANCIAL SERVICES

Only 4% of customers think banks have a good understanding of customer experience and 62% of customers think that their banks don't listen to feedback and take action.

70% of customers worldwide are willing to provide their bank with more information if this leads to greater personalization or better service.

IBM WATSON
At your service

Fundamentally transforming the way people and companies interact and build relationships.

Consumers will interact directly with Watson to get timely, accurate, personalized responses to inquiries.

Understand the subtleties of human language

Search through vast amounts of Big Data

Deliver fast, evidence-based answers to users' questions

RETAIL

Enterprises in the U.S. lose an estimated $83 billion each year due to defections and abandoned purchases as a direct result of a poor experience.

Research shows that 86% of consumers will pay more for a better customer experience, and 89% of consumers began doing business with a competitor following a poor customer experience.

TELECOM

47% of telecom marketers will focus on retaining relationships and building stronger affinity with existing customers in 2013.

40% of telecom marketers plan to improve the relevance and value of communication and content in 2013.

Source: Courtesy of International Business Machines Corporation, © International Business Machines Corporation. Reprinted with permission from IBM Corporation.

The natural language processing and learning ability of IBM Watson can:

Predict new trends and shifting tastes: Watson processes enormous amounts of consumer data and learns as it goes along. It does not forget anything: data from credit cards, sales databases, social networks, location data, web pages, and it combines all the information to make high-probability predictions and even sentiment analysis. Interestingly, Watson can recognize irony and sarcasm—and find out the intended meaning. This ability helps it to quickly analyze large sample sizes to determine whether a product offering or clothing line will be accepted by consumers.

Analyze social conversations and thus generate leads: Watson can predict what information is most important and go through reports about the industry, competitors, partners, and customers and make recommendations on how to act on it. For example, if it finds some people discussing problems, it can match those with the company's product and notify the sales team.

Determine whether a new innovation will sell or not: Watson can learn from one domain of knowledge and make high-probability predictions in another, and this helps it to understand whether a new innovation will sell or not. It crunches the company's current market and customer base to provide success probabilities, as well as provides a sharp picture of the opportunities and threats.

Computer-calculated and automated growth hacking: Growth hackers seek to maximize conversions on e-mails, websites, social media, online content, or other digital media. Watson does this to measure and optimize digital content, ads, website pages, and even a company's product to maximize customer growth.

Measurement of ad effectiveness and media planning: Nielsen has partnered with IBM Watson to improve measurement of ad effectiveness and media planning. Its data-parsing system is used for CRM, customer call centers, and other purposes through its

Watson Engagement Advisor offering. Questions like *who are my best prospects in a category* and *how much should I budget for next year* are answered by taking into account data that might be normally ignored. By identifying prospective customers, ad effectiveness will become more efficient.

Data trails are analyzed in a series of five steps. Starting with finding out what people need, it also helps to identify focused advertisements, tailor-made promotions, reinvents purchase experience, and finally encourages positive WOM (Figure 5.1).

How these are achieved is discussed in detail here.

Identifying Consumer Needs

Big data helps right from the beginning, that is, by identifying consumer needs. Predictive analytics track data from various sources to tell companies what people need before they know it.

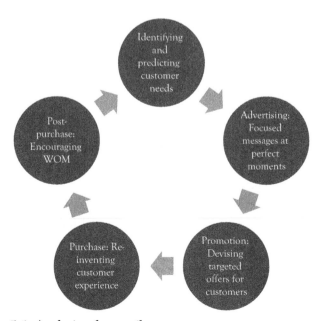

Figure 5.1 Analyzing data trails

The information that earlier took years to collect and analyze is available easily today. Take a look at how data trails lead to the consumer's mind:

- Cookies on computers and social profiles reveal the consumer's income bracket, age, sex, and education.
- The Internet address can reveal the consumer's geographic location right up to their address. Mobile devices using GPS reveal the exact location of the customer.
- The kind of device used reveals the consumer's affluence: for example, Apple computer owners are likely, on average, to be better off than Windows PC users.
- What people write or share on various websites reveals about their personality and emotional state.
- Clicking behavior shows consumer needs: for example, someone clicking too quickly to check out means that the consumer has already decided to buy, so no discounts may be offered.

All it requires is a good detective, or a data analyst, who can make sense of these trails and combine them with data streaming in from various connected devices.

Focused Advertising

In advertising, companies create microfocused targeted messages that are delivered at the perfect moment, when the consumer is receptive toward receiving such ads. Data analytics help discover which ads will be most liked and should be served to individual customers.

This is a big help to companies because traditional ways of advertising do not work anymore. Mass media is fragmented today and losing its effectiveness, which is described by Bob Garfield as *The Chaos Scenario* (2009) in the book of the same name. "Newspapers, magazines and especially TV as we currently know them are fundamentally doomed," he predicts as audience shrinks globally. Connected consumers prefer to fiddle with their connected devices rather than listen to what the media is telling them. How marketing communications can be made more relevant is discussed in Chapter 6.

Devising Offers

Just as ads can be precisely targeted, so also can products. Companies track what a consumer likes across the Internet and are able to modify their offers. Using consumer data with online tracking, nowadays companies are able to create customized offers that immediately attract customers. Davenport, Mule, and Lucker (2011) call these *next best offers* (NBOs). Based on social, mobile, and location information of customers, "companies are beginning to craft offers based on where a customer is at any given moment, what his social media posts say about his interests, and even what his friends are buying or discussing online," they write.

New methods of understanding customers are being developed. One such method is Real-time Experience Tracking (RET), which helps companies to know how and which touch points influence the consumer decision journey most significantly. The method involves asking a consumer panel to send four-character text messages through their mobile phones when they come across a brand or a competitor during their purchase process. The short message sends the codes for brand, touch point type, positivity or the feeling of the customer, and a rating of persuasiveness. Qualitative details are captured when respondents are surveyed about their brand-attitude changes.

RET helps companies to track effectiveness of ads, track competitor stimuli, and more importantly, helps understand how consumer attitudes change over touch points during the purchase journey. The sequence of text messages of RET reveals insights that traditional surveys cannot reveal.

- Unilever used this method to find out about the effectiveness its Axe campaign in two countries. Though its TV advertising in Italy and Poland was positively received, the company found the brand was not doing very well in Italy but was a huge success in Poland. Through RET, it found that in Poland, the ads followed street experiences in which an *Axe*

Police consisting of attractive women would *arrest* young men and spray them with Axe. The company found that using such experiences at touch points greatly increased the effectiveness of advertising.

- A charity found that the in-store experience of donors was not very good, so donations were getting affected. It decided to use a smarter layout and displayed messages about its work, and this resulted in increase in donations.
- PepsiCo relaunched Gatorade in Mexico. By using RET, the company found that advertising and touch point experiences in gyms and parks were twice as effective as doing it in stores. Shifting ads and distribution into these touch points resulted in a successful launch.

Dialog, access, risk–benefits, and transparency are emerging as the basis for interaction between the consumer and the firm, which helps in reinventing the purchase experience for customers.

Reinventing Purchase Experience

Traditional retailers had a big advantage over today's companies—they knew about their consumers. A person running a small store could recognize most customers, engage them in small talk, and make gentle product recommendations. Companies and retailers do not have this luxury today, but now big data promises to give them the same advantage. As customers walk into a store, their mobile phones give away their identity and location. If they are already using the store's app, the company immediately knows their profiles and purchase history. This data can be used to enhance consumer experience and also to generate loyalty. Companies can now deliver convenience just like the traditional small retailer in the following ways:

- Engage with customers as they walk in and react to their needs through real-time data;
- Deliver personalized service and product recommendations;

- Increase sales by helping customers at the point of purchase by frontline employees armed with tablets; and
- Integrate physical and online activities to influence consumers at all points in their decision journeys.

The retail store then becomes much more than a place to browse and buy. It becomes an opportunity to deliver a personalized experience; the store and the online presence become one entity. Argos, a UK retailer, has a *digital first* strategy through which it places self-service iPads which customers use to browse product videos and reviews. The store provides free Wi-Fi to help customers use their own devices to check prices and products. While customers are happy to get free Wi-Fi, the store benefits as it gets tracking data to help in personalized promotions. Dynamic digital screens have replaced traditional posters and display screens. It offers a 60-s fast track service for customers who have ordered online.

Big data provides an indispensable arsenal for companies consisting of:

- *Apps*: Allowing the customer to get online easily increases the possibility of consumers downloading the company's app. The app helps the company to start a two-way communication with the customer. More importantly, it helps the collection of consumer data that can be used to track and to send messages or deals. Customers use apps to scan bar codes to access product information whenever they want, seek opinions, and order for home delivery.
- *QR codes*: QR code walls are used in the store or at busy places like subways through which passers-by scan codes for products displayed on screen. Products thus ordered are delivered at home or through a click-and-collect service, depending on the preference of the customer.
- *Mobile payments*: Mobile payments help customers, sparing them the need and hassle to carry cards or cash and to remember the codes required to authenticate payments. Apps now link bank accounts and allow consumers to pay

by smartphones. Customers can also check themselves out using apps.

- *Digital signage*: Digital signage displays not only product information but also QR codes and the number of *likes* an item has received on Facebook. Virtual reality mirrors can display images of what garments will look like on customers and allow them to share those images with friends over social media. Burberry stores use radio frequency identification device (RFID) chips embedded in clothing that help customers with information on mirrors in changing rooms.
- *Beacons*: Stores are also employing beacons, which are small Bluetooth devices that can communicate with customer smartphones, when they are near or in the store. Beacons help to track customers and deliver offers. For example, if a customer passes a store without visiting it, a reminder or a coupon is sent that helps them pull him or her back into the store.
- *Empowering sales staff*: Stores can gain perhaps the most by empowering frontline staff with tablets. They provide information and show products and catalogs to customers on their tablets, compare prices, take orders, help them to check out from anywhere in the shop, and so on. Restaurants help people scan menus and order on tablets even as they are waiting for a table. More important, frontline staff can access customer information by using Bluetooth devices.

Postpurchase: Encouraging WOM

WOM is one of the most important factors in purchasing decisions, especially for a first-time purchase. Its influence is growing with the digital revolution: Today every experience or comment is shared with friends. Digital WOM is read by many people, and product reviews and opinions play an important role in purchase decisions: It is no longer an intimate, one-on-one conversation, but one-to-many communication because clever reviews and comments have the tendency to go viral.

Social data analytics involves real-time tracking of what is posted on social sites. Moreover, it requires going beyond the surface and analyzing the context in which the comments are made: The analysis has to uncover sarcasm and statements using double meanings. This calls for sophisticated data and text analytics. IBM reports that such tools are available today, which are as follows:

- *BigSheets*: BigSheets help to crawl the Web and analyze massive amounts of data on social sites.
- *Text Analytics*: Refers to the process of deriving high-quality information from text. The software quickly finds information buried in unstructured text data and understands its context and content.
- *IBM Watson*: Computer analysis of natural language posts (see Exhibit)
- *Semantic enrichment*: Analytics help to understand the context of human speech and thought.

Social media is the single largest source of WOM. But monitoring it and encouraging consumer engagement is tough because it spans the three dimensions: Gartner calls big social data as consisting of three Vs: high-volume, high-velocity, and high-variety information. Social data is huge: more than a billion consumers spending about a quarter of their time on social media platforms. The speed at which the social data flows is remarkable too: It is available in real time or nearly real time. It is constantly refreshing, providing quick and accurate insights into what people are doing or liking, if only we have the means to listen. And then, there is variety. Social media provides different kinds of data such as images, videos, and text. Companies can encourage WOM through the following ways:

- *Content engagement*: By tracking how users interact with content, including shares, referrals, and participation in social campaigns, companies can track trending subjects. Skillful companies can interject such trends with their own compelling content.

- *Fan loyalty*: Companies also have the means to track how frequently fans interact with their posts and campaigns and can identify opinion leaders. Such insights can lead the way to offer exclusive programs and offers for brand advocates and increase the effectiveness of brand content.
- *Fan interests*: Fan interests and interactions provide clues about consumers' intention to purchase.
- *Social profile data*: Social profile data helps in segmentation and consumer profiles give away what interests people, so as to engage them.
- *User-submitted data*: User submitted data is integrated with data about their behavior and interests to run targeted campaigns and get people talking about them.

While data analytics is a goldmine for companies, there are some limitations to it as well. It is important to keep in mind what data cannot reveal as well.

What Data Cannot Reveal

Many writers explain that big data analysis is a paradigm shift and enables companies to move away from gut feelings and toward data-driven decision making. While this may be true, can the human element in marketing be truly ignored?

Lee and Sobol (2012) write that human behavior is nuanced and complex, and data can provide only part of the story. Desire and motivation are influenced by a number of factors that have to be understood in context and conversation. "Data can reveal new patterns that point a firm in the right direction, but it can't indicate what to do once there. It reveals *what* people do, but not *why* they do it," they write.

For instance, if you notice a person with an eye movement, you can probably make out whether it was a wink or a twitch. But data cannot. When *customer intelligence* is applied to consumer behavior, companies are likely to find that knowing about someone is not the same as knowing them. Customer data can be used to strengthen customer relationships, but those actions have to build values and trust. Enamored with the predictive power of data, we often lose out on how to deal with people. Systems generate e-mails, SMS, and telephone calls to customers by millions, which are merely seen as intrusion in personal lives. Sending a birthday greeting to a customer might seem good CRM by a company, but for a customer getting such a message from a nameless and faceless company may mean nothing at all.

Secondly, many companies do not have access to big data analytics. Meer (2014) writes that small companies, companies in emerging markets, and business-to-business (B2B) industries operate in data-sparse situations. Such companies have to *adopt a series of little data techniques* to develop solutions for their needs.

A word of caution is given by Ross, Beath, and Quaadgras (2013). They warn about the hype surrounding big data which has made companies expect more than they can. Very often managers can gain insights merely by observing people. Moreover, using data analytics requires huge changes in business models and organizations that companies are either incapable or reluctant to do.

In the ultimate analysis, data analysis cannot substitute for common sense and observation. Companies also have to learn to use little data as well, which requires three things, writes Meer:

- *Orientation fact-based decision making*: Companies have to adopt fact-based decision making, which is the basis of competitive advantage.
- *Learn by doing*: Many business decisions are taken by trial and error. When little data starts yielding results, it can inspire people to learn by doing.
- *Using creativity*: Then there is creativity. Marketing is a creative task, in which consumers like to be surprised and delighted. It is doubtful that merely relying on data analytics can encourage the managers to approach their jobs creatively.

In the next chapter, we discover the marketing communications that affect modern consumers like Mary. Data techniques, farming social media information, help to create targeted communications which people do not block out.

CHAPTER 6

Marketing Communications for the Connected Consumer

Mary hardly ever looks at the newspaper and her attention while watching TV is divided. But she loves social media, where all her friends are. How have communications changed to target people like her?

There is a revolution in marketing communications. Though mass media remains the vehicle for reaching a large number of people, the fact that people prefer to interact with their own little screens is changing the rules of the game. Can companies elbow into this personal space and introduce their messages? Or create compelling reasons for people to visit their sites and thereby become loyal to them?

To achieve this, companies have to align their messages and content with what people are doing online at a specific time. If either the message or the timing is inappropriate, people will see it as intrusive and irritating. The unwanted tweet or an unwanted friend request will most likely be blocked out, and sometimes will invite a consumer backlash as well. That is why online communication has to be used with great care and understanding.

A Better Way to Advertise

The idea, therefore, is to send relevant messages at the right time, rather than sending unwanted spam messages hoping that someone will see them. The benefits—in terms of reduced wastage in advertising expenditure—are huge. But then companies have to engage customers when they are most receptive, writes Rayport (2013). In his article, *Advertising's New Medium: Human Experience,* he writes that big data helps advertising to engage consumers in four spheres:

- *Public sphere*: The sphere in which a person moves from one place or activity to another. Ads in this sphere have to be relevant in context, help people, and be compelling.
- *Social sphere*: Activities in which people interact with each other; ads in this sphere must address a social need or facilitate interactions.
- *Tribal sphere*: The sphere in which people connect with groups. Ads in this sphere will provide means to empower consumers for self-expression, status, or affiliation.
- *Psychological sphere*: In this personal sphere, companies try to link brands to a personal value or emotions.

In his blog post, Rayport gives the example of Diageo, which ran a pilot program on Father's Day in which consumers could scan product codes on individual bottles of spirits by their mobile phones and create videos for dad and upload them. The recipient dad could download the video, thereby leading to increased personalization of the brand experience. Such activities redefine advertising in at least five ways:

1. The advertising message is placed into everyday social life.
2. The gift giver creates a message which also serves as a crowdsourced advertising for the firm.
3. Users can personalize products through unique codes.
4. Products become smart to deliver dynamic ad messages.
5. It builds consumer relationship with the brand both online and through physical products.

Two methods, *dialog marketing* and *programmatic ads,* represent great strides in communicating effectively with consumers.

Dialog Marketing

Data analytics help to place focused ads to consumers that they find interesting and deliver at a time when they most need them. This is done through a computer-based model called *dialog marketing*. Kalyanam and

Zweben (2005) explain that *dialog marketing considers not just when to communicate but also how to communicate.*

Through dialog marketing, companies continuously track loyalty indicators by traditional recency, frequency, and monetary value (RFM) scores in real time. The system tracks a transition in this score the moment it happens and launches a dialog with the customer. Data is collected at all touch points, which is then used to customize marketing messages and personalize the experience. It is an interactive model that tracks many communication channels, following each customer's interaction with a company. Kalyanam and Zweben (2005) describe how new methods of tracking customers as given below can generate dialogs with them:

- *Intelligent process engines*: These engines track individual *states* of a consumer, that is, a consumer's relations with a company at a point in time. Action is initiated based on changes in these states.
- *Event-driven computing*: Intelligent engines continuously *listen* and track what customers are doing, and decide when to react, initiating dialogs when the customers are most likely to respond.
- *Scalable web architecture*: Scalable web architecture makes it possible to track volumes of dialogs as they increase.
- *Web services*: Multiple data systems must talk to each other. This technology makes it possible to connect dialogs and to listen to customer activity in real time.

Programmatic Ads

Programmatic ads link real-time data to ads based on what a person is doing at that time. The platform allows companies to participate in split-second auctions to be able to present an ad to a customer on the basis of data from various sources such as his or her browsing history, purchase behavior, social media usage, sociodemographic profile, location, and other criteria. Many variants of ads are created and the one matching individual customers are displayed on their screens through dynamic variation.

Apart from advertising, companies have to become adept at using social media, where the customers are. Its importance has increased in recent years.

Importance of Social Media Communication

Social media is where consumers are. Companies eye clusters on social media spaces because they want to be with their customers. Today, customers flock to social media sites and companies flock after them, trying to get them involved with their brands. It is the dream of every marketing manager to get the attention of millions of people who log on to such sites everyday to listen to their messages.

But the task is not easy because of two reasons: first, they have to understand what people do on social media, and second, they have to deal with different screens and platforms. As pointed out in a report by Nielsen (2014), in many countries, people spend an average of 60 hours a week consuming content across multiple screens—that is about eight hours every day. Two-thirds of the people surveyed said they used social media sites at least once a day. Indeed, social networking is somewhat of an addiction. Increasingly, people use two screens at a time, showing the importance of a multichannel approach.

Companies thus struggle to understand how to get people involved with their brands on a platform which is essentially social, not commercial. They try to understand things like:

- What do people do on social media? How to get people on social media engaged with brands?
- Why do people seek out a company or brand on social media?
- What makes a customer willing or reluctant to interact with brands online?
- Does social engagement really result in increase in sales or loyalty for a company?

- How can social media be used to assist marketing strategy of a company?

Answering these questions helps companies to facilitate collaborative experiences and dialog that are relevant to customers. Simonson and Rosen (2014) write that communication must match the consumers' influence mix, derived from the sources of influence on the consumers' decisions—prior experiences, influence of other people or of companies. There are two mistakes made by companies while using social media: first, it is treated as a persuasion tool, like other media, and second, it still uses old concepts of marketing. Online executions, however, must be done with a different purpose and intent.

Online Communications

Many companies make the mistake of trying to add numbers online, and this is often useless. For instance, campaigns to get viewers to see a video on YouTube, to get visitors to a website or to get *likes* on Facebook may do nothing for a brand. Such traffic can also often be manipulated. Similarly, online advertising is often blocked or directed to spam folders.

Traditional ways of thinking about advertising campaigns do not work. Piskorski (2011) writes that most companies do not succeed on online social platforms. Though they try to use social media, few companies succeed in generating profits on social platforms, despite collecting lots of *friends* and *followers*. The efforts by companies to connect with consumers on social media are rejected *because their main goal is to connect with other people, not with companies*, he writes. Though there are many firms giving advice on digital marketing, little of it goes beyond building traffic and getting people to "like" brands.

Campaigns encouraging *likes* will only go that far; people may like a brand on social media for its content, but continue buying another because it better suits them. Many companies have started *me-too* pages on popular social sites and even managed to collect a large number of fans, but converting them into paying customers remains an uphill task.

Digital marketing suffers from the fact that few people combine data skills with marketing skills. Knowledge is divided into two distinct camps:

1. On one side are advertising and marketing professionals who understand advertising, marketing, and branding, but are clueless about incorporating social media with their brands.
2. On the other side are the social media enthusiasts who know everything about sharing content and collecting fans but are completely lost when it comes to branding, marketing, or developing consumer loyalty.

That is why most social communication media strategies fail. Stauffer (2012) writes that social media are at odds with the traditional campaign mindsets that are still used in many planning models. As a result, too many marketing and communications programs on social media are *social* in name only, with the vast majority of resources spent managing the flow from brand to consumer and little or no meaningful consumer insight affecting the way the business operates. Most brands lack a process for ensuring a balanced mix of social media-led planning both downstream to consumers' lives and upstream to business objectives.

Big data offers a way to send targeted communications, integrating online and offline requirements of consumers, as summed up in Table 6.1. The idea is that online communications should drive online sales or store sales, while store visits by customers are made more informative and profitable by providing real-time information and offers.

It is seen from Table 6.1 that communications have to take the best of online and offline methods. Big data enables companies to get inside the lives of their customers, figuring out what problem is sought to be solved. *Mobile moments* help companies to figure out what is beneficial for the consumer at a particular moment and, thus, gain relevance.

Several companies have been successful at combining customer needs with online communications.

- Uber connected people wanting a ride to drivers who were in that area and could carry a passenger.

Table 6.1 Online executions of different communications tools

Communications tool	Online executions
Advertising	Programmatic ads, ads that take into account a person's location and need, virtual storefronts and displays
Selling	Sales persons as information providers through tablets; real-time tracking, identifying opportunities to engage and sell, virtual sales staff
Sales promotion	Based on customer's location and needs, offering online incentives and rewards, loyalty schemes, below-the-line (BTL) activities in the physical world
PR	Online editorials, e-zines, newsletters, discussion groups
Sponsorship	Sponsoring online and offline events
Direct mail	Focused e-mail and web response
Exhibitions	Virtual exhibitions
Merchandising	Virtual interfaces, shopping malls, e-tailing
Packaging	Displays QR codes, links to product information
Word of mouth (WOM)	Enabling customers to share experiences through free Wi-Fi in stores; viral, affiliate marketing, links, social media
Social media	Customer engagement

- Bank of America allows customers to deposit a check in their accounts by taking a picture of it.
- The Delta app lets people rebook flights while standing at the gate.
- In some countries, McDonalds lets people to place their order while walking to the restaurant.

Companies have to get over their habit of one-way communication with customers. Instead they have to embrace social customer relationship management (CRM), which facilitates collaborative experiences that engage customers.

Social CRM

Social CRM is the CRM built by communication with customers through social networking sites. It is social media that is the engine for users, which is used by organizations to get people engaged through strategies that encourage social CRM (Figure 6.1). Greenberg (2010) explains that social CRM is *the ability of a company to meet the personal agendas of customers while, at the same time, meeting the objectives of its own business plan. It is aimed at customer engagement rather than customer management.*

Social CRM is based on the understanding that:

- *People do not look for brands on social media*: Social media is not used as a search engine for brands. It is a social platform where people engage with each other. They may also look for product opinions and reviews. Only engaging content that fits into customer needs can get them engaged with brands.
- *People use social media to connect with friends and family*: Social networking is about personal connections with friends and family. These personal connections are trusted and valued. Merely pushing products through them will be rejected.
- *Companies need to develop passion for brands*: Companies hope that people will talk or comment positively about their brands or experiences with them, but people who feel passionate for a

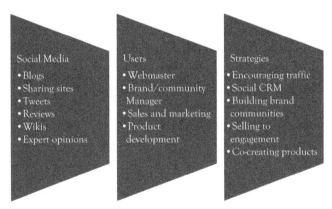

Figure 6.1 Engagement strategies through social media

brand will only do so. Marketing activities encouraging brand passion must be clubbed with online activities.

Successful Strategies

Social strategies only work when consumers can connect the marketing effort to their lives (Exhibit 6.1). According to Piskorski, companies' intervention in the social space should help meet some social objectives such as:

1. Reduce costs, or solve customer problems by helping people meet and connect;
2. Help connections, establish or strengthen relationships, and thus increase willingness to pay or to reduce costs; and
3. Encourage customers doing free work for company, such as WOM communications, assisting in product development, and so on, by instilling a sense of achievement for them.

If done properly, social media communications can fulfill several objectives of businesses and lead to engagement strategies. The brand manager tracks sites to spot and mitigate negativity, while the community manager encourages engagement to get people talking about brands and products. Webmasters look for referrals and try to get people sharing contents and links that lead to their website. Product development managers use social media to understand and analyze shifts in purchase behavior and try to involve consumers in the product development process. Using social media, consumers are linked to manufacturing in real time.

Exhibit 6.1

Best Customer Engagement Campaigns

Brand communications must combine mass media and social media channels now. They must engage users and provide triggers for action. Some of the best campaigns of 2014 which won the Mashies Awards are described in this section. Each of these succeeded in integrating communication channels and also involve people with brands through social media.

1. *Burger King Cheat on Beef:* Burger King wanted to encourage consumers in New Zealand to *cheat on beef*, that is, change their habit of consuming beef burgers to chicken ones. Using an audacious cheating theme, it converted a motel into Burger King Motel by changing the signage and placed branded accessories such as robes, towels, stationery, and towels in it. The beds in the rooms were replaced with booths where people could try out the new burgers.

   Adopting an irreverent tone, it promoted the concept through humorous TV commercials. People were required to book a room on its Facebook page. Four friends were assigned a booth where they could *cheat on beef*. People were encouraged to check into the motel through their Facebook accounts and try out the new burgers. They were encouraged to share their experiences and pictures using the hashtag #motelBK. In this way, the company got over the resistance people have to share branded messages and instead created the need to share their unique brand experiences. The campaign was a success as it got user-created content and quickly became viral.

2. *AT&T's SummerBreak*: In an effort to reach out to young consumers, AT&T combined three channels for its campaign, @SummerBreak: reality TV, social media, and mobile phones. The reality series is about eight smartphone using friends having their last memorable summer break together before college.

   Viewers had to follow the program's Twitter feed, as well as the feeds of the participating teens using AT&T's devices, which provided them links to videos and other content. The series collected a large following on YouTube, Twitter, Instagram, Tumblr, Vine, and Snapchat. The company posted short episodes on Tuesdays and Thursdays and a 20-min episode was posted live every Sunday, collecting 20 million views. Keeping it authentic, the content did not have traditional TV ads or phrases like *powered by AT&T* or *brought to you by AT&T*. The 51-episode series became so successful that AT&T launched a second season in June 2014.

3. *Tombstone's Bites of Fright*: Tombstone Pizza wanted to reach mothers and children to make it *the official pizza of Halloween*. Building on the tradition of families watching a horror movie over a pizza together during Halloween week, the company made 31 six-second videos for every day during the month of October 2014. Featuring friendly clips of spooky characters, the clips were posted on Vine, Twitter, and Facebook. To involve families further, it created Facebook posts called *Crunch-time Costumes* in the Halloween week, which gave ideas for clever last-minute costumes. On Twitter, it used the hashtag, #bitesoffright. The campaign quickly became viral. Figures on Social Media Practices showed that it achieved a virality rate of 23× and a 230 percent increase in Tombstone's fans on Facebook.

4. *Chevy and the American Cancer Society Paint Social Media Purple*: Chevy launched an emotional *Purple Your Profile* campaign which paid tribute to cancer survivors. Using a moving 60-s spot at the 2014 Super Bowl entitled *Life*, it asked people to change their Facebook profile to *purple* and pledged to donate one dollar to the American Cancer Society for every person who participated. The campaign became hugely popular, with over 1 million people changing their profile to purple. Consumer brands like Energizer and Lowe's joined the movement.

5. *Nestle Coffee-mate's Stirring up Love Outside the Cup*: Nestle's Coffee-mate used Valentine's Day for its social campaign. Partnering with professional artists, it helped turn users' declaration of love into shareable valentines. Using the hashtag #CMValentine, it allowed consumers to submit love notes on Twitter and Facebook. The company turned the posts into hand-crafted Valentines which could be shared with friends. The *outside the cup* idea took expressions of love into miniature works of art, which added to consumer engagement. In this way, the company succeeded in engaging its followers and added new ones too, encouraging people to express how they felt. Since Valentine's Day is popular, the campaign became very relevant to consumers, adding a cherished moment to their romance.

Major Shifts

There are five major shifts that have occurred in marketing communications due to the connected nature of consumers and companies.

1. From campaign management to social CRM;
2. Help consumers find brands;
3. From selling to engagement;
4. Relationships between touch points and
5. Building brand communities.

These strategies are explained in this section.

From Campaign Management to Social CRM

Traditionally, communications are thought of as campaigns which provide leads to sales. Social CRM goes beyond managing campaigns to building engagement and relationships. The strategy focuses on engaging customer in collaborative conversations. This is called social CRM. Along with advertising in the mass media, companies have to focus on getting customers involved with brands online.

A Nielsen report, *How Digital Influences How We Shop Around the World* (2012), says that companies still have to learn to use social media as it is a two-way communication medium and they must engage in the dialog to stay in control. The report describes how social CRM can help companies to do the following:

1. *Focus on the right shopper.* Companies can first focus on the active users of social media. Nielsen found that about 25 percent of shoppers can be considered as *trendsetters*, or people who love to keep ahead, try new things, and tell others about them. Focusing on such shoppers will build opinion for others to join in.
2. *Engage shoppers with the right message.* The message should fit in with a consumer's need to be relevant. Companies have to determine activities that are important to core shoppers and customize their messages.

3. *Connect with shoppers via the right medium.* Companies have to communicate via the right medium: Physical stores have to be matched with mobiles and apps, salespersons are to be armed with tablets, and shopping has to be made easier. Companies today cannot limit themselves by medium since people move between their devices seamlessly.

Help Consumers Find Brands

Today consumers find brands, rather than the other way around. The efforts of companies have to be on getting into consumers' Moments of Truths. This represents a paradigm shift in marketing practice: shifting from targeting customers to engaging them. Berger (2013) has given six key principles (STEPPS) that can help customers find brands, talk about them, post comments, and include them in the decision journeys. Note that there is no distinction between online and offline worlds when the objective is to get people talking.

1. *Social currency*: *Social currency* describes communications by people to create positive impressions about them. Talking about *cool* products or ideas, posting pictures with them, and getting likes on their posts make people feel good. Companies have to try to get people talking and posting about products in their social posts. They have to create social currency through quick attention and responding to queries or by giving them exclusive deals. Customized products also make people feel that the company is giving importance to them, which helps in sharing products in social communications.
2. *Triggers*: Triggers are things that get people talking. WOM is triggered by what people see or experience. Triggers have to be built in communications so that people associate brands with experiences and share them. They have to be repeated frequently, but the danger is that too many reminders may put off customers.
3. *Emotion*: Berger says that information alone does not get people to act; emotions do. People share experiences if they feel emotionally moved or highly aroused. So, companies need to arouse them by

linking emotions such as awe, excitement, amusement, anger, or anxiety with their brands.

4. *Public*: People tend to copy others. Called the *mirror effect*, it helps brands spread virally. As people see others using brands or products in public, they get influenced to buy or talk about them. Brand managers, therefore, have to find ways to make people use their brands and products in public. Or, if they cannot be used in public, creative labeling helps to spread the word, such as labels put on luggage of guests when they check out of a hotel, or the famous *Intel Inside* sticker on laptops and computers. Amazon offers *share your purchase* button by which people can post purchases made on its site on social media sites. Online companies send their products in distinctive packages so that others see them and get influenced to buy from them. Flipkart encourages people to use its packaging for other uses such as making dustbins so that they are visible to others.

5. *Practical value*: Another way of building social currency is by offering value: People like to help others or show off brands if they think they have got exceptional value in buying them. Major triggers are saving money, personal achievements like losing weight or looking good, or planning a vacation to an exotic destination. Group purchasing sites like Groupon are built on the assumption that people like to share value with their friends and buy in groups to avail discount.

6. *Stories*: Stories are another way to get people to participate and feel important. Great stories are shared by people, especially if they feel a part of it. Companies thus create brand stories or share unique customer experiences to get people talking. Instances of quick response to customer comments are of solving customer problems, amplifying referrals and recommendations, and fostering communities help spread stories.

From Selling to Engagement

The efforts of companies have to be on getting consumers engaged with brands, rather than selling. Customers can be engaged by contributing to firms in many ways beyond transactions. Companies have to encourage nontransactional active interactions with their customers.

Customer engagement is being recognized as *a more strategic way of looking at customer and stakeholder relationships* according to the Economist Intelligence Unit (2007). Whereas earlier, engagement was limited to developing better CRM, now the relationship is sought to be deeper and more meaningful.

If a brand can develop an emotional connect with its users, engagement via social platforms becomes easy. However, because brands are not people. It has to be done with a genuineness of purpose, by listening and responding to consumers, and by involving them. As Greenberg (2010) explains, "Human beings love to participate and create." It is up to companies to harness this desire of people. Successful companies understand that the customer is not just a source of sales, but wants to actively participate in value creation with business. Technology provides a number of ways that companies can join with their customers to co-create value.

The framework for engagement includes a four-step approach:

1. *Plan*—The communications plan must specify what is to be achieved. The objectives have to be specified in terms of key performance indicators in the social media space.
2. *Listen*—Companies have to track in real time what is being written and talked about on the Internet. Conversation hotspots give clues about when to intervene in conversations. Listening also helps to know changes in loyalty parameters so as to initiate dialogs at just the right moment.
3. *Analyze*—Conversations are analyzed to understand consumers, their emotions and motivations, and their response to brands.
4. *Engage*—A creative approach is needed to engage customers and to form the best platform and medium upon which to build relationships.

Above all, the engagement has to be based on trust and sincerity. Commercial messages do not work because the engagement is seen as artificial. If social media users perceive a company's messages and intentions as sincere, they will engage with brands. Care has, therefore, to be taken that the communications do not become one way or are blatant attempts to sell, because people are quick to block such attempts on their phones, e-mails, or feeds on social media. Social media is not about driving sales, but about making emotional connections, exceptional service, and engaging conversations.

Prahalad and Ramaswamy (2004) write that companies that want to succeed in this new era need to experience their businesses as consumers do, and through *experience networks*, they can co-create better products and opportunities. This cannot happen without bringing about deep changes in how managers and leaders think. The marketing paradigm, which thus far was focused on company or brand, is outdated and needs to shift to *customer think*, which leads to a difficult but necessary sharing of information at all points in supply chains right up to customers.

That is to say, brands have to operate like interesting people whom their customers would like to know. Since friendships in the real world are based on sincerity and trust, companies too must develop these qualities in all their communications.

Relationships Between Touch Points

Companies have to look for specific relationships between touch points, and find out how users flow from one point to another. Today communication strategy has to track changes in consumers' feelings as they move between touch points and initiate dialogs. Dialog marketing, which tracks changes in RFM scores and triggers dialogs with consumers, has been described earlier in this chapter.

Dialogs are designed to guide the customer to new transactions or to develop a deeper level of engagement. Since dialogs are initiated when the customer is in a particular mood or transition, attention is guaranteed. For instance, a consumer looking at cooking devices in a store can be guided to particular brands or sections by sending a personalized message.

Marketing managers today have the means to initiate dialogs with lightning speed to capture the mood of the audience with split-second accuracy. Consider the following examples:

- When there was a brief power blackout at the Super Bowl in 2013, companies responded with alacrity—Oreo tweeted, "Power Out? No problem. You can still dunk in the dark."

Tide tweeted, "We can't get your #blackout, but we can get your stains out."

- When London had a hot summer, Wall's used the opportunity to send advertising messages to city residents about its ice cream. In cold weather, Kleenex used Google ads to target areas where people were most likely to catch a cold.
- Microsoft sent e-mail offers for its search engine Bing, which gets tailored to the recipient in the 200 milliseconds when it is opened. When a person opens the mail, the user's real-time information is used to tailor the offer. As a result, conversion rates improved reportedly by 70 percent.

Such messages not only got smiles from the audience, but also resulted in high brand recall. They encourage consumers to engage with it because they are relevant.

Brand Communities

Brand communities are built on the understanding that people who consume a particular brand have affinity with each other and share common interests. A brand community is a group of consumers that shares social relationships based on usage or interest in a product, and is therefore a means of building engagement. Sometimes it is made by consumers themselves; at other times, it is made by a company. It is based on attachment of consumers to a brand—the stronger the brand, the stronger is the brand community. Events and get-togethers are organized so that consumers meet others who share their enthusiasm for the brand.

Customers seek variety, entertainment, and belongingness through brand communities. If they are passionate about the brand, they will join such communities, online and offline. The secret is to make people feel valued. They are also based on honesty. Communications must, therefore, include authenticity and trust, on all devices, all the time. Hudspeth (2012) writes that the secret lies in two simple philosophies— engage people through relevancy and provide them with value, while being transparent and authentic. These objectives are met through brand communities.

Brand communities encourage C2C communication. Fournier and Lee (2009) explain, "In today's turbulent world, people are hungry for a sense of connection; and in lean economic times, every company needs new ways to do more with what it already has." A strong brand community, they write, increases customer loyalty, lowers marketing costs, authenticates brand meanings, and yields an influx of ideas to grow the business. Strong brand communities result in better returns through commitment, engagement, and support.

Beyond social interaction, communities encourage passion. Evidently, consumers will interact only with brands they know and love. McWilliam (2000) writes that for brand relationships to be cultivated over time, companies have to devise communication that:

- Customizes messages for individuals;
- Rewards the individual for fostering the community; and
- Strengthens the relationship between people and brands.

Sometimes brand communities evolve into movements and encourage creation of tribes. Consumers make communities themselves—as the creation of fan pages and chat groups on social media sites. Many websites are integrated with such communities, so that people can share things they like on them on social media sites. Indeed, many brands, such as Starbucks, Coca Cola, and Ikea, have used brand communities to engage consumers through social networking. But this is not the rule: A study by Socialbakers, which gathers social media statistics, found that 95 percent of posts to brands' pages on Facebook went unanswered. Any interventions by the company that are not natural or are commercial in nature will be squarely punished.

Love–Respect Axis

Social media has resulted in redrawing the business communications for firms. The lines between producer and consumer are today blurred: The company and the customer are operating in conjunction with each other.

The second aspect of the new business model is a change in thinking from campaign-specific to customer-centric approach. Different metrics are required; instead of measuring traffic from social media sites, companies must learn to look at how social performance helps to shift key performance indicators, such as brand value and sentiment, customer retention and satisfaction rates, apart from sales and profits. The campaign-oriented thinking of the past cannot be used in media which is essentially controlled by consumers.

But does this imply a change in approach? For years, brand managers have known that great brands are built on love and respect of consumers. CEO of Saatchi and Saatchi, Ken Roberts (2004) described a *love–respect axis*—which he wrote worked "best in conversation: conversations about product and brands ... conversations about successes, conversations to spark insights." Brand equity was built on emotion, optimism, quality, trust, and stories. By building on passion points—music, fashion, sports, celebrities, entertainment, and technology, brands could earn the love from their consumers.

CHAPTER 7

Measuring Web Equity

Companies are keen to measure the spending and value that customers like Mary are actually worth. Traditional methods of customer lifetime value (CLV) have to be augmented to measure engagement and word of mouth (WOM) values as well.

We have seen that customers today have more power than in the past because they have more information and control over the communications, but in return willingly give more data to companies. This chapter looks at value created both for customers and companies and how it can be capitalized for mutual benefit.

Traditionally, companies have attempted to measure value by assessing customer acquisition, retention, and loyalty through measures like customer equity and CLV. These in turn are based on measures like sales revenue, profitability, market share, and depend on the transactional nature of customer relationships.

In addition to transactional data, companies now have access to data streaming from social media, location data from sensors, digital data from browsing habits, and traditional market data. Real-time analytics combine traditional metrics and social data with data from multiple sources to yield marketing information. The various types of data and its measurement are summed up in Table 7.1.

Traditional metrics are available faster, and moreover, the data can be analyzed better slicing and dicing it through better tools. New metrics can be developed by using the streaming data that helps in managerial decision making. Both traditional metrics and contemporary metrics are summed up in Figure 7.1. Companies can make dashboards for various functions and monitor data in real time.

We, therefore, need better metrics to measure all these data that are available today. A big challenge is to measure social data, which is qualitative in nature but which holds the key to understanding consumer behavior.

Table 7.1 How different types of data contribute to customer value measurement

Transactional data	What a customer is buying and at what time Measuring recency, frequency, and monetary value (RFM) Patterns of purchase Customer acquisition, customer activity, customer win-back Share of the wallet, CLV
Location data	Age, income, social status, leading to better market segmentation Microtargeting consumers
Digital data	Search engine data, browsing habits, e-mail
Social data	Analyses of posts on social media, tracking likes, dislikes, comments, brand shares Personal data for microtargeting Customer referrals, influence, engagement value Sentiment analysis
Sensor data	Weather, volumes, sales forecasting, in-store behavior of customers Geo-targeted advertising Product operating information from customer sites
Marketing data	Market share, sales growth, segmentwise sales analysis

Measuring Social Data

A big advancement in consumer data metrics is tracking social information that people willingly share on social media sites. This is the key to understand consumer engagement. Increasingly, social content measuring systems are becoming available for companies to track this vast and wild space. Some common tools to monitor social media involve tracking engagement, reach, and consumptions.

Engagement shows the number of people who are engaged with the brand's online activities. This figure gives an indication whether the audience is actively involved with the brand or not and shows the following:

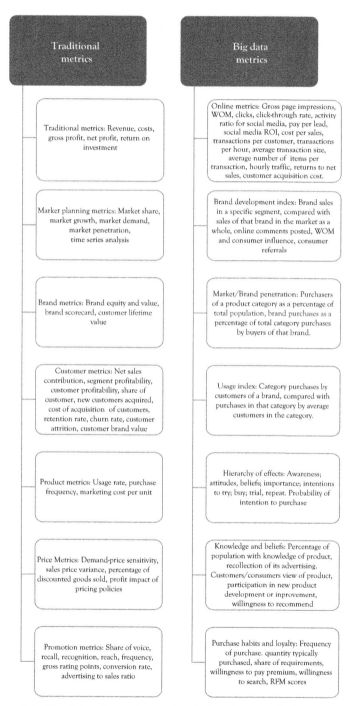

Traditional metrics

Traditional metrics: Revenue, costs, gross profit, net profit, return on investment

Market planning metrics: Market share, market growth, market demand, market penetration, time series analysis

Brand metrics: Brand equity and value, brand scorecard, customer lifetime value

Customer metrics: Net sales contribution, segment profitability, customer profitability, share of customer, new customers acquired, cost of acquisition of customers, retention rate, churn rate, customer attrition, customer brand value

Product metrics: Usage rate, purchase frequency, marketing cost per unit

Price Metrics: Demand-price sensitivity, sales price variance, percentage of discounted goods sold, profit impact of pricing policies

Promotion metrics: Share of voice, recall, recognition, reach, frequency, gross rating points, conversion rate, advertising to sales ratio

Big data metrics

Online metrics: Gross page impressions, WOM, clicks, click-through rate, activity ratio for social media, pay per lead, social media ROI, cost per sales, transactions per customer, transactions per hour, average transaction size, average number of items per transaction, hourly traffic, returns to net sales, customer acquisition cost.

Brand development index: Brand sales in a specific segment, compared with sales of that brand in the market as a whole, online comments posted, WOM and consumer influence, consumer referrals

Market/Brand penetration: Purchasers of a product category as a percentage of total population, brand purchases as a percentage of total category purchases by buyers of that brand.

Usage index: Category purchases by customers of a brand, compared with purchases in that category by average customers in the category.

Hierarchy of effects: Awareness; attitudes, beliefs; importance; intentions to try; buy; trial, repeat. Probability of intention to purchase

Knowledge and beliefs: Percentage of population with knowledge of product, recollection of its advertising. Customers/consumers view of product, participation in new product development or improvement, willingness to recommend

Purchase habits and loyalty: Frequency of purchase. quantity typically purchased, share of requirements, willingness to pay premium, willingness to search, RFM scores

Figure 7.1 Traditional metrics and real-time data analytics

- The brand's ability to capture users' attention;
- Effectiveness and relevance of the brand's content; and
- The number of people who see and share the content.

Engagement leads to increased brand awareness, because consumers' actions appear in their social media posts, making the brand visible to their friends. Engagement also gives an indication about the types of content that the audience is interested in. This helps in creating such content that is liked by target customers, and also provides insights into the interests of consumers.

Engagement and engagement rate can be calculated as follows:

Engagement = likes (or website registrations) + comments + shares

Engagement rate = total engagement (likes + comments + shares)/ total fans

Engagement rate is calculated by expressing the number of people who liked, commented, tweeted, shared, or clicked on a brand post as a percentage of the number of people who saw the post. It helps to measure a company's effectiveness at engaging the audience. It shows the types of posts that are most likely to be shared or commented upon and the quality of content created.

Reach shows the number of unique people who have seen the content. There are three types of reach: organic, paid, and viral. *Organic reach* refers to the number of unique people who see the content on their own. *Paid reach* is the number of unique people who clicked on advertisements or paid content. *Viral reach* refers to the number of unique people who saw the post mentioned in a post published by a friend.

Measuring reach by type can help companies pinpoint the factors that contributed to content views. Organic reach is the result of increase in number of fans or their increased engagement. Viral reach shows whether the content interested the consumer enough to be shared by them. Paid reach shows how effective the ads are. Reach shows the brand's effective audience and is a more accurate measure than views.

Impressions are the number of times the brand content is displayed and seen by consumers.

Organic impressions refer to the number of times the content was displayed in a user's page. *Paid impressions* consist of the number of times the content was displayed as a result of online advertisements. *Viral impressions* show the number of times content was shared or commented upon by a friend: it shows liking, commenting, sharing, or answering a question or responding to an event. The key difference between impressions and reach is that impressions measure the number of times the content was displayed, while reach measures the number of unique people who saw the content.

Stories include updates from friends, including likes, engagement, sharing, joining, tagging, and so on.

Stories associated with a brand show how posts are effective in driving awareness for brand content.

Consumptions consist of clicks anywhere in the post. Clicks can be on links, photos, videos, and so on. Measuring the number of clicks on posts provides a complete view of engagement as it shows what users are interested in. The click-through rate for each post or content type allows a company to measure the frequency of engagement with its content. The people who click on any of the posts are called *consumers*. They can be segmented by the type of engagement action taken.

Sources are the locations of people who liked the brand or content or who registered on a website. Sources can be viewed on the brand's page, ads, or posts.

These analytics help in the following ways:

1. *Measure the audience actually reached*: Reach, which measures the unique number of people who saw the content, can give a good idea of the audience who saw the content.
2. *Analyze engaged users*: Engaged users are the people who took action on the content. Companies should try to grow this audience.
3. *Create context for fan growth*: New fan growth serves as a community health indicator and to organically increase audience size too.
4. *Identify engaged customers*: Location metrics help to identify engaged customers. Their demographics provide precise information about them.
5. *Discover when customers are most active*: When people interact with brands gives an indication to companies as to when is the best time to reach them. This helps to cater precisely to market needs.

However, the limitation of tracking social media by the above methods is that it measures audience reactions to *content* rather than marketing and sales. Post an interesting or funny video, for instance, and people will see it, share it, and rave about it—but will they buy the product the next time? Indeed, the usage of the word *customers* in the above context is wrong, since people who are engaged with brands online may, in fact, never buy the product. The above measures of engagement merely show whether the content posted by a company is liked by people or not. The only advantage that companies can gain out of such social media tracking is that the brand becomes known and may be considered if and when the person wants to buy the product. What is required is quantifying new visitors who selected the brand because of the content seen. It is here that big data analytics can help, as it goes beyond measuring the response to brand content.

Exhibit 7.1

Nestlé's Digital Acceleration and the Human Element

Nestlé is a global food company with over 2,000 brands, including such household names like KitKat and Nescafé. With such well-known brands, it faced the problem of tracking what consumers were saying about it: The task involved monitoring 170 million fans across social media sites. How could the company possibly track and respond to what these fans were posting about the company and, that too, all the time?

To do this, the company has set up a digital acceleration team (DAT) at its headquarters in Vevey, Switzerland, to monitor conversations about its products on social media. Online sentiment is tracked in real time on screens showing how people respond to its brands. It also trains its marketing leaders from around the world in an eight month program in digital and social media. Through an entrepreneurial and open-source setting, they learn to manage communities for the company's global brands. After training and thought leadership, they go back to work in digital or traditional marketing, carrying what Pete

Blackshaw, global head of digital marketing and social media at Nestlé, calls *digital vitamins*.

The DAT has four principles: listening, engaging, transforming, and inspiring. Using a social content management system with tools such as Buddy Media, Vitrue, or Wildfire, the company is able to monitor the wild space of social media. Apart from tracking brands, it engages in community management and content production. Through its training, the company produces next-generation brand leadership— global brand managers who understand both brand fundamentals and digital engagement. DATs have been established in India, Italy, China, and other countries.

Tracking consumer digitally also helps in the following:

Publicity: The teams at DAT help generate publicity online. A French team member, for instance, developed an app that plays a cookery video when a package code is scanned. Perrier sales were helped by a video which became popular on YouTube, with the storyline: To save a melting world, a glamorous woman drinks Perrier.

Adaptive marketing: Adaptive marketing is using real-time signals to create and modify marketing inputs. Tracking consumers digitally helps in experimentation, quick execution, and changing gears to maximize marketing return on investment (ROI). Nestlé's brands are thus changing from mass marketing approaches to social—they sense consumer sentiment and respond to it. The company realizes that consumers want to engage with brands on social platforms, and DAT helps in this.

Dealing with negative publicity: Digital acceleration helps to tackle negative comments posted by consumers. Nestlé has faced consumer anger for its use of palm oil (leading to destruction of rain forests) and its water bottling business (exploiting free goods), reports Reuters (Thomasson 2012). Ignoring such issues tends to make them larger: the press amplifies them, and they are shown in search results across the world. DAT monitors negative comments about the company's brands as they are posted: the center's screens turn red if a negative issue is emerging, alerting the teams to engage and respond when a high number of negative comments are being posted online.

Connecting internal social media: Nestlé has one of the largest internal social networks with 200,000 users. It has created communities such as *Winning with Mobile* and best online listening practices. Recruitment and relationship building are facilitated through such platforms. This also creates agility and flexibility in the system.

However, technology only goes thus far. Finally, it is human element that makes a difference. In 2015, Nestlé faced a disaster as its best selling noodles brand, Maggi, was found to contain excessive levels of harmful substances. The company failed to respond in the first few days and let the crisis balloon. As a consequence, the brand had to be withdrawn from the market, showing the human failure despite its data analysis capabilities.

Market Research and Big Data

Big data analysis consists of tracking much more than social media. It involves tracking data from diverse sources using advanced tools. Court, Gordon, and Perrey (2012) write that companies have to ask some basic questions so as to improve returns on marketing spending. These questions relate to the following:

- Finding the exact influences on consumers;
- Financial efficiency in marketing plans—how accurately are they hitting a small, moving target with highly focused messages;
- Monitoring how fast the organization is responding to customer comments; and
- Measuring the impact of multiple communication and marketing channels.

Because of data-based marketing, companies can quantify and measure—often in real time—the results and impact of their efforts. Earlier, managers had to wait for a few months to find out how their efforts impacted markets and consumers, which could only be known when the monthly or quarterly sales figures came in. Similarly, how consumers reacted to products could only be known through extensive surveys which not only took time but also suffered from researcher or consumer bias. Today, however, every action can be assessed almost immediately, as Nestlé's DAT initiative shows (Exhibit 7.1). A product, its usage, or a promotion scheme can be tracked, for instance, by monitoring social media and tracking how many people are talking about it or sharing it with their friends. Similarly, by linking segmentation data with logistics and supply chains, a company can know how well different groups of customers are being served.

To be effective, marketing metrics must meet the following three requirements:

- *First,* the ability to link a company's internal operating system with streaming data from outside. This involves breaking silos and developing networks of influence and collaboration.
- *Second,* the need to use the present market research tools to develop new tools to meet the needs of high volume, high velocity, and high variety data.
- *Third,* the need to bridge the data creativity link so that human creativity continues to drive marketing with the appropriate data rather than reducing marketing to a mere set of numbers.

As we have mentioned earlier, this calls for complete transformation of the business model. Once they are geared toward making full use of data, they must develop marketing metrics which give quantitative indicators that help in achieving:

1. *Focus*: Metrics serve to measure marketing and advertising objectives, and thereby provide the direction and focus needed on key

performance criteria. While earlier, the focus had mostly been on financial results like sales and profitability, today it has shifted to consumer engagement, branding, and discovering drivers of consumer action.

2. *Better vision*: Monitoring data gives better vision to companies, or provides them the ability to spot threats and opportunities faster.

3. *Better decisions*: Tracking metrics helps in making better decisions. Managers need not rely on intuition or whims, but on firm evidence.

4. *Better performance*: Big data drives profitability. *Companies in the top third of their industry in the use of data-driven decision making were, on average, 5 percent more productive and 6 percent more profitable than their competitors*, shows a research conducted by Andrew McAfee and Erik Brynjolfsson (2012).

Using big data metrics requires radical changes in the way companies are organized and managed. This change in thinking and approach has to percolate at all levels of organizations. Yoram Wind (2008) gives seven strategies that serve to increase the rigor and relevance of marketing research in times of big data.

1. *Bridge disciplinary silos*: Big data marketing and metrics entail breaking down of disciplinary silos in organizations. Integrating functional departments is not only essential to deliver customer experience but also to measure marketing ROI. "Markets can be seen through either a behavioral or quantitative lens, but as with binocular vision, we gain more depth when we look through both," writes Wind. There is need, therefore, to bridge the great divide between behavioral and quantitative approaches. Second, marketing and other disciplines too have to break down barriers between them. Technology experts, for instance, have to work with marketing managers to develop systems that serve one or the other objectives of serving customers. Third, sophisticated models of data-driven results must not obfuscate the need for creativity, intuition, and subjective judgment, so essentially required in marketing.

2. *Network orchestration*: The shift toward network orchestration from traditional management thinking requires another big shift in approach: Managements have to develop capabilities to build and manage networks, called *network orchestration*. Instead of optimizing the company, managers have to think about optimizing both the company and its network, since competition is increasingly *network against network*. Further, instead of strong control systems that exist in hierarchal organizations, managers must learn to rely on empowered employees, partners, and customers.

3. *Customer managed relationships (CMR)*. Through traditional customer relationship management (CRM), companies try to make relationships with their customers. But the connected era requires a shift to *CMR*, that is, to encourage customers to develop their own relationships with companies through platforms that allow customers to engage with them. Sites that encourage customers to post reviews on hotels, movies, and travel do not focus on selling products, for instance, but give consumers power to publish their views and thereby get involved with the sites.

4. *Customer branding*. Brand power is increasingly shifting into the hands of consumers. Companies have to let brands evolve through codeveloping, coproducing, and comarketing with their customers. This may be difficult for managers and companies who have the mindset of controlling their brands, but the trend is growing.

5. *Real-time analytics and metrics*. New measures to track and evaluate investments in marketing are needed, and these are provided through analytics. Real-time data provides changes in consumer sentiment as it happens. Further, data analysis looks at drivers of consumer behavior and changes in RFM scores as they happen in real time.

6. *Adaptive experimentation*: *Adaptive experimentation* combines research and action: Companies conduct marketing experiments and immediately incorporate the creative insights and perspectives generated into action.

7. *Challenge mental models*: Finally, there is an urgent need to change old mental models for marketing. Empowered consumers have

never existed before, so managers need to change mental models to comprehend and utilize this radical shift in marketplace.

The above shows a huge shift in thinking in company managements, which is essential if companies have to manage the many ways in which customers add value to them.

Some companies have indeed succeeded in breaking traditional marketing mindsets and are using data analytics creatively for many diverse tasks.

Target: An article in *The New York Times* (Duhigg 2012) shows how Target uses data. It records all consumer activity by an individual: using credit cards, coupons, surveys, refunds, calling the customer helpline, e-mail, and visits to the website, linked to demographic information such as age, family size, location, salary, and online behavior. Using easily available data, it can know about ethnicity, job history, magazines read, financial history, personal life, and topics that interest individuals. Using *predictive analytics*, it knows not just a person's shopping habits but also what he or she is going to need next, developing a basis of efficient marketing and micro targeting.

eBay: eBay conducts a wide variety of activities such as machine learning, data mining, economics, user behavior analytics, information retrieval, and visualization using big data. Data from a wide variety are integrated: user, user behavior, transaction, items, feedback, and searches.

GE: GE uses big data analytics to predict the maintenance needs of its jet engines, turbines, and medical scanners. It is using operational data from sensors on its machinery and engines for pattern analysis.

Amazon: Amazon mastered the recommendation of books, toys, or kitchen utensils that their customers might be interested in. Other companies have followed suit, such as recommending music on Spotify, movies on Netflix, or pins on Pinterest.

Delta Airlines: Delta Airlines identified customers' pain points: All airlines know a top concern for passengers is lost baggage. The company looked further into their data and created a solution that would remove the uncertainty of where a passenger's bag might be. Customers can now snap a photo of their baggage tag using the *Track My Bag* feature on the Delta app and then keep tabs on their luggage as it makes its way to the final destination. Even if a bag does not make it on the intended flight, passengers save time tracking it down.

As shown by the aforesaid examples, leveraging big data capabilities can help to form instant strategy decision, spur innovation, inspire new product and services so on, and build competitive advantages besides building customer relationships. Capturing and measuring this value calls for new approaches that are described in the next section.

Measuring Customer Value

Modern times require that companies harness data from multiple sources and monitor them simultaneously, writes Kevin Lindsay (2014). The key performance indicators must be measured across multiple internal and external sources. For example, Lenovo analyzed consumer satisfaction to find out why people were phoning the call center. By analyzing data from six sources, the Web, postpurchase surveys, CRM system, call center, e-mail, and live chat, it could find out the issues that customers called for. This was rectified by providing better content on its website, and the company was able to reduce customer calls and dissatisfaction arising out of call waiting time.

All metrics have to be focused on deriving lifetime value. Roland Rust and his colleagues (2010) explain, "Companies must shift their focus from driving transactions to maximizing customer lifetime value."

A number of metrics are drawn together into dashboards that give an integrated picture of marketing events as they happen. Real-time metrics can be monitored through dashboards, enabling the linking of marketing to other departments or activities. A customer's decision journey, for instance, can be tracked by a dashboard that shows how he or she was influenced, then following the order within the company to logistics till it is received. This simple journey requires linking together data from multiple sources, but gives information on how quickly the company responds to customers and how satisfied they are. Finally, the impact of monitoring the consumer decision journey is measured on sales, profitability, and growth. In other words, marketing activities related to influencing consumers can be directly linked to profitability.

Customer Engagement Value

A method is needed to put a value to the many ways that customers add value to a firm or destroy value by posting negative comments and reviews. One measure is suggested by Kumar et al. (2010), which is the customer engagement value (CEV). According to the authors, CEV offers a complete measure of how much a customer contributes to the value of the firm in terms of four components:

1. *CLV*: CLV is a commonly used indicator and is calculated as the sum of the present value of future profits generated from customers over their lifetime. It helps companies to estimate about the future profitability of individual customers and the products that must be launched to meet their needs as they move from one stage of their consumption to another. It also measures purchases made by individual consumers and provides stimulus for building loyalty and repeat purchases. Since CLV is the sum of purchases by consumers, it also provides opportunities for up-selling and cross-selling. The metrics used for CLV are share of the wallet and the present value of expected lifetime spends of customers acquired.

2. *Customer referral value (CRV)*: When customers influence their friends and family members through sharing of experiences and positive comments, they add value to the firm. Companies encourage such behavior by rewarding existing customers to bring in their friends and acquaintances through referral programs. CRV measures the value of such referrals by estimating the number of successful referrals, or new profitable customers that existing customers add. CRV is calculated as the number of customers acquired through referrals and their expected lifetime values.

3. *Customer influencer value (CIV)*: Consumers influence others either directly by persuading and converting acquaintances into customers

or indirectly by persuading strangers to adopt products when they see someone using the product or brand. New products can get a boost by direct and indirect customer influence, which adds to a person's CIV. Firms can estimate their CIV by quantifying the number of reviews posted, the number and lifetime value of customers acquired from influence, opinion leadership through the number of followers, and use of social media and blogs.

4. *Customer knowledge value (CKV)*: Another way that customers add value to the company is by participating in knowledge development—that is, when they participate in developing new products or provide other kinds of feedback that helps company know insights into behavior or usage. For instance, market research becomes much easier when customers voluntarily share information, as opposed to undertaking expensive surveys. Brand communities encourage sharing of knowledge to those who participate in them through common problem solving and having product-related discussions. Ideas contributed by customers for improving existing products and service delivery also add value to firms. The metrics used for CKV are the number of meaningful interactions with the company, suggestions and participation in new product development by customers and its value.

In the era of the connected consumer, both brand awareness and brand image are a function of referrals, influence, and knowledge.

Calculating Customer Equity

Customer equity can be measured in several ways. The traditional measure is CLV, which gives the lifetime value of customers. But new methods are needed. The share of the wallet, voice of the customer (VOC), and WOM equity approaches are given below.

Customer Lifetime Value

CLV is the total combined expected CLVs of all of a company's customers. It is calculated by estimating the expected contribution of customers over their expected life and discounting the values to a net present value and summing them up. It is shown mathematically as

$$CLV = \sum_{t=0}^{T} \frac{(p_t - c_t)}{(1+i)^t} - AC$$

where p_t = price paid by customer, c_t = cost of servicing customer, i = discount rate, and AC = acquisition cost.

Share of the Wallet

Keiningham et al. (2011) give the concept of the share of the wallet, which calculates the percentage of a customer's spending of a brand within a category of products.

Voice of the Customer

The VOC approach measures a customer's feedback about his experiences with products or services. It gathers multisource information about consumer conversations about brands and products online, such as blogs, forums, wikis, and other spaces, which can be done through natural language analysis and text processing from social media channels. VOC analytics shows actionable insights on a dashboard. The VOC approach can give deep insights about customer preferences, their feedback, trends, and early warnings from social media conversations. It is based on three activities:

- *Listen:* Social conversations about the brand or company;
- *Analyze:* Identify root causes and sentiments; and
- *Correlate:* Combine with internal data and surveys to give feedback and actionable points.

WOM Equity

Bughin, Doogan, and Vetvik (2010) show that WOM equity should be calculated by companies. It is given by multiplying average sales impact of a brand message by the number of WOM messages. The sales impact is based on three things: what is said, who says it, and where it is said. Companies assign scores on the type of messages posted, the influence of the person who posts the message, and the context in which it is said. WOM equity measurement helps companies to test the effectiveness of how brand messages are created and shared.

By developing metrics for different aspects of engagement, firms arrive at a measure to estimate the sources of value of their connected customers: their profitability, the value of their referrals, influence, and the contribution they make toward improving existing products or ideas for new product development.

Newer metrics will be developed to measure customer value. "Measuring value in the era of the connected customer requires that we measure share of hearts, minds, and markets," write Farris et al. (2006) in their book, *Marketing Metrics: 50 + Metrics Every Executive Should Master*. It involves measuring customer perceptions, market share, and competitive analysis. Transactional data, combined with market segment data, sensor data, and consumer data delivers a comprehensive dashboard that helps measure marketing ROI.

CHAPTER 8

Future of Consumer Behavior

Mary loves the ease and fun of being connected. In fact, she cannot imagine a world when people were not connected. She is quick to respond to and adopt new technologies. She often wonders what new delights would be invented in the future. There is a niggling fear in her mind—will her profiles and pictures be hacked, or used by an unscrupulous person or organization? She gets concerned with every report of hacking and even leaking of celebrities' profiles. She had read a book sometime back—1984 by George Orwell— in which all information about people was controlled and used by an autocratic government. She wonders whether the future will be a consumer utopia or will it be an Orwellian nightmare, where everything we do will be watched, tracked, analyzed—and manipulated?

In the movie *Eagle Eye*, two people are shown to be manipulated to do dangerous things by a computer that tracks them and controls their every move. Eagle Eye is also the name of a company and the film makers probably chose the name because the *multipatented transaction software platform, supporting real-time, multichannel digital offers, vouchers, and rewards*, as explained on its website, matched the core idea of the movie.

Though the film was a science fiction, it has a scary scenario in which people's data is used to manipulate them—a scenario that is very close to becoming reality at least as far as data availability goes. Using software to make offers to customers is fine, but the movie showed that data analysis can be misused by anyone who has the expertise to correlate different sets of data.

Schmidt and Cohen (2013) make a prediction in their book, *The New Digital Age*, "Soon everyone on earth will be connected." For companies, it will bring big gains in productivity as it will give them a means to understand consumers better. For consumers in rich countries, it gives more convenience, access to a wide variety of goods, delivered very fast. In developing countries, it will mean helping millions of poor and scattered people without access to government or financial services to get out of poverty. Connectivity will help improve inefficient markets by bringing producers and consumers in contact with each other, reducing waste and improving efficiency. For consumers in such countries, connectivity will also be a means to access products and services that they do not have access to.

As consumers, we may like having our lives made simple by companies which track our habits and movements and practically all personal information. Wearable devices track our moods and heartbeats as well, telling companies how we feel. On our screens, there is endless content available, and robotics and voice recognition provide seamless forms of engagement with technology, easing the availability of products and communication across borders.

Unfortunately, all this convenience comes at a price. The technology that gives us ease through connectivity also gives the power of data manipulation to individuals and companies. As we try to look into the future, the ease and simplicity of buying products may also sow the seeds of an Orwellian nightmare. In this chapter, we try to map consumer behavior of the future and also identify the fears that data availability evoke.

Retail of the Future

We have seen in the earlier chapters that new ways of serving customers can be devised using new technologies. As data analysis becomes widespread and getting information about consumers becomes easy to farm, companies will be able to integrate the physical and virtual worlds. Retail will be helped by spontaneous availability of information. Some of the changes in business models are described in this section.

Integration of Online and Offline Worlds

We are already witnessing changes in both consumers and companies. Consumers compulsively check their phones and feel deprived if Internet access is not available. They check products and prices across channels on their phones even as they visit retail stores. Companies, on the other hand, realize that online tools must be used in integration with their physical facilities and structures. Online-only stores will thus move into the physical world, setting up stores where customers can experience, touch, and feel products, while brick-and-mortar stores will add online channels and treat their physical stores as delivery channels for orders obtained online.

Personal Lives No More

Consumers use the Internet as an extension of their lives. Bell (2014) explains in his book, *Location is (still) Everything*, "What we are finding is that the way we use the virtual world of the Internet—for commerce and for information—is dictated to a large extent by the physical world that each of us resides in." Companies will find more ways of getting into their lives to offer solutions. When they do so, the lines between personal and public will get increasingly blurred.

Efficiencies in Retail and Logistics

Integration of channels will result in greater efficiencies by cutting down on inventories held at various points in their marketing channels. For expensive products like cars and white goods, this holds much potential. Car showrooms, for instance, will have no cars to show: Consumers see and feel products on 3D imaging technology instead of physical products. They can experience the cars on simulators and then place an order on screens while selecting their preferences. Such things are already a reality. The Audi store in London delivers a virtual experience of every possible combination of the Audi range. The company's website says, "Audi City is a new digital car showroom format that uses state-of-the-art technology to make clever use of precious city space." The company delivers brand experience digitally, and saves on car inventories in showrooms and instead uses digital presentations to present the cars on huge screens. Visitors check out and select the interiors and exteriors, listen to the sounds of exhaust and opening and shutting of doors. The store also has paint, wood, and leather samples which can be viewed and touched. Customers use hand-held tablets and can configure a car and view their creation on the big digital walls. Companies thus save not only on inventories, but on real estate costs as well. In addition, it allows the brand to spread to new markets where it does not have dealers.

Online Companies in Physical Spaces

Online companies, on the other hand, will find—as many have already found out—that finding customers online and then servicing them is too uneconomical. Many will be forced to shut down: For instance, many start-ups just could not achieve the scale and economy of operations and had to be shut down. Companies will, therefore, use online interactions to deliver information and guide customers to the nearest retail stores, instead of online ordering. Creative solutions will thrive.

Crowdsourcing and Co-creation

The trend toward crowdsourcing and co-creating products will only increase. Creative ways of using consumers to help companies with design, production, and publicity will multiply.

Many new technologies will evolve to help e-commerce and for making the lives of customers easier.

New Technologies

Many technologies and databases are already being used to track customers and improve business efficiency, such as radiofrequency identification (RFID), digital displays, digital mannequins, magic mirrors, touchscreen kiosks, virtual fitting rooms, and 3D printing. Many others will become available in the future. Some of these technologies have the potential to be disruptive technologies, holding the promise of significantly reshaping the shopping experience.

RFID

RFID is used to identify and track objects by means of tags attached to them. These tags, about the size of a rice grain, consist of a small chip and an antenna. The chips contain electronically stored information, about 2,000 bytes of data or less, which is enough to identify objects. They have no power source, and are tracked either by electromagnetic induction or by reflecting radiofrequency. This makes them cheap. Since they use reflection of energy waves, they do not have to be within the line of sight of the reader. Embedded RFID tags are thus an efficient way to track inventories, vehicles, and even people and serve for Automatic Identification and Data Capture.

In production lines, such tags are used to track the progress of a package or product through the assembly line. Movement of physical goods can be tracked in supply chains and retail stores, while livestock and pets can have identification and tracking through RFID tags. In retail, they can enable automated checkouts and inventory tracking in real time. Such tags can be used as:

- Security tags for products;
- Web address for any product information;
- Virtual labels, assembly instructions, repair instructions, replacement, recycling, and so on; and
- Better inventory management from throughout the supply chain.

Digital Displays

Digital displays are used in stores and in high traffic areas (such as subway stations) to display products and codes that consumers can scan with their mobiles and place orders by connecting instantaneously with company or review websites. The displays change every few minutes to attract customers, and products displayed change with the time of the day. Digital signage precludes the need for opening a store and will significantly reduce real estate costs. Customers can simply take a picture of the products on the display screens and order while on the move.

Digital Mannequins

Digital mannequins are projection video images and allow retailers to display more products much more effectively than traditional manne-quins. The images can be life-size or larger and create great impact as the mannequins move and change poses, in different outfits. The technology can revolutionize retail by displays that grab customer attention. Many companies are already using this technology, including Tesco, which entices customers by a virtual mannequin that appears to be speaking to customers and tapping on the window.

Magic Mirrors

The magic mirror is an intelligent photo booth with an interactive screen through which customers can see how they would look in different dresses. Deploying a plasma screen and a depth-sensing camera, it allows people to *try on* different fashion items available in the store by merely tapping on the screen. The mirrors use 3D technology to superimpose clothing items over a live picture of a customer. Employing movement sensors technology from gaming applications, magic mirrors judge the consumer's size and adjust the size of the dress at the wave of a hand.

Consumers can check the latest fashion items without going to a store and searching for suitable products. Products are changed by tapping the screen, which also allows customers to adjust the lighting to see how they will look in different conditions. Magic mirrors will do away with changing rooms in stores, since they allow consumers to try on different dresses, sizes, and colors without actually changing clothes. Once the purchase decision is made, payment is made by simply tapping on the magic screen. Many stores are already using this technology, including eBay.

Self-Service Touchscreen Kiosks

Self-service kiosks allow customers to browse and make purchases from product lines available in-store and also the extended ranges available online. Orders can be collected from the store or delivered to homes. Barcode scanners allow customers to look for product ratings, reviews, and suggested accessories. Combined with augmented reality technology, kiosks can be used to generate a life-size 3D image of the product scanned from a catalog.

Virtual Fitting Rooms

In virtual fitting rooms, customers enter their basic measurements and a virtual mannequin is created for dimensions. Alternately, a 3D scanner is used, which takes over 3.5 million body measurements to create a virtual mannequin of the exact body size as the customer, which can then be used to try out various dresses and accessories. Technologies such as magic mirrors and virtual fitting rooms are able to get the exact size of the person, thus reducing the returns rate. It is helpful for customers too, as they can try out all types of dresses and variations suitable for their body type without trips to the changing room.

3D Printing

3D printing—in which consumers can *print* objects from a computer design—promises to dramatically change the way business is conducted. The technology is already making a dent in industrial design. 3D printing has the potential of reinventing supply chains by reducing inventories held by retailers and dealers. Stores of the future may well have no physical goods at all, but large displays and virtual models showing the products, which consumers can modify to their tastes and can then *print them out* even as the customer waits.

Also known as additive manufacturing, it is a technique in which products are built layer by layer using a computer-driven, additive process. It can build plastic and metal parts directly from computer aided design (CAD) drawings that have been cross-sectioned into thousands of layers. It is possible to *print* out an object using these drawings in the same way as we use printers these days. Retailers thus reduce their investments in finished goods and offer a far broader array of customized products. 3D printers may lead to mass customization of consumer goods in the future, and, connected with a database of designs, would open a number of possibilities such as the following:

- Many products would not be stocked, but made as and when needed, leading to efficiencies in production and supply chains.

- Products could be customized for individual customers and inventories reduced to zero.
- Quick product development and prototypes would lead to shorter lead times for product development and speed to market.
- It gives the freedom for anyone to become a designer, making fast fashion even faster.
- In developing countries, people can print out whatever tools they require to improve their productivity.

Mass customization offers the ability to produce custom output, combining the low unit costs of mass production processes with the flexibility of individual customization. According to *The Economist* (2011), "Three-dimensional printing makes it as cheap to create single items as it is to produce thousands and thus undermines economies of scale. It may have as profound an impact on the world as the coming of the factory did."

All these new technologies add up to a utopia of unlimited goods and choices, fulfilling needs in a jiffy. These and other technologies will continue to evolve, giving more and more choices to consumers and tools for better efficiency to companies. But technology is a double-edged sword. These same technologies accumulate data about consumers, making us all in effect into naked apes.

Consumer Utopia or Naked Ape?

Easy availability of information and infinite customized choices forms the ultimate consumer democracy. But all this convenience comes at a price. The information shared by consumers is used in a myriad of ways to help them, but this very information poses loss of privacy as well. Already, some consumers feel stalked, with some of their most personal data used by companies to target them. People do not mind as long as it is used to offer products or services, but increasingly, the information is being used in ways never intended (Exhibit 8.1). Big data can combine different data sets to pinpoint individuals in their most personal habits.

In his book, *The Black Box Society*, Frank Pasquale (2014) writes that companies track our personal behavior by scrutinizing clues that we leave online, to create incredibly detailed portraits. The problem arises because there are no checks about what firms are doing with this information. "Hidden algorithms can make (or ruin) reputations," he says. The book calls for controlling powerful interests that abuse information for profit. But whether any legislation or moral concern prevents data misuse remains doubtful.

In the digital age, will humans become the naked ape, to borrow a phrase from Desmond Morris? Are we going to become mere cogs in the data machine? As people realize this, will they be comfortable with the idea of sharing information online?

Exhibit 8.1

Stalking Customers

Your very personal details, habits, and inclinations are known not only to companies but also to governments, and can be accessed by hackers and antisocial elements. By combining commercial data with public records and mobile data, anyone can play havoc with your life.

This is not a science fiction anymore. In their article in *The New York Times*, Tufekci and King (2014) write that a senior vice president of Uber threatened to expose the personal lives of journalists who were critical of the company. The threat showed that Uber had sensitive data on people: The company had claimed in a blog post in 2012 that it knew about people who possibly had affairs—they took *rides of glory*, that is, went somewhere other than home on Friday or Saturday nights. By tracking customers, Uber knew exactly where their customers went. Further, it had a *God View* to stalk VIP users.

If Uber has all this information, one can well imagine what smart companies like Google and Facebook know, or even the government, which has powers over these companies. In 2013, Edward Snowden leaked records that showed how the U.S. government was also in the act. A telecom company was shown to be sharing data on call duration and location with the government. A program called PRISM was shown to collect *e-mails, files, and social networking data from firms such as Google, Apple, and Facebook* (*The Economist*, June 15, 2013b).

Add predictive analytics to the brew and companies know what illnesses you are likely to have, what your outlook is, and whether you should be kept under police watch for a crime that you are likely to commit in the future. Big Brother is not only watching you, but knows your future as well!

People do not realize that behind the ease of shopping that they experience is a science that tracks their every move. Data can become convenient to creepy in the following ways, writes Schloss (2014):

1. *Stalking*: We know that companies follow their customers everywhere and track every online movement. If customers start perceiving it as stalking, they will avoid doing business with such companies.
2. *In poor taste marketing*: By tracking customers, algorithms make product suggestions, which often results in marketing in poor taste. For example, if a person has lost someone and does an online search to find a funeral home, he will be flooded with offers pertaining to caskets, gravestones, and floral arrangements, even after the event is over. Such targeting is in poor taste, because it reminds customers of their loss.
3. *Misuse of data*: The third element is misuse of data, which means that someone uses data for ulterior reasons. A health company sharing information about a client with an insurance company is misusing data. Uber threatening journalists and stalking VIPs is another misuse of data. Yet, such misuses are happening today.

Humans in the Data Machine

This brings us to the question: Is there a limit for big data analysis for consumer analysis? Or will our existence become bits and bytes in a big analytical marketing machine? Will human judgment have a role to play, or will companies know everything about us and send us things as and when we should need them? Will shopping be reduced to some clicks on our mobile phones or thought-directed commands on wearable devices?

This is an imaginable scenario. But it also ignores the fact that shopping has always been a multidimensional affair—people like to hang out with friends, check products, browse shop windows, and walk the High Street. We buy many things on impulse, for the sheer joy of catering to our desires. All shopping is certainly not merely recognizing needs and following a series of steps to fulfill those needs. "Human behavior is nuanced and complex, and no matter how robust it is, data can provide only part of the story. Desire and motivation are influenced by psychological, social, and cultural factors that require context and conversation in order to decode," write Lee and Sobol (2012).

The authors give the example of a wink, which can be interpreted as a signal or a mere twitch. That meaning can be understood only by a human who understands the cultural and emotional significance, and not by data analysis. Indeed, some instances of embarrassing customers by using data have been reported as follows:

- Data analysis of purchase patterns revealed that a girl was pregnant. She was sent offers for pregnancy-related products, even though she had not disclosed the fact to her family.
- A patient received a call reminding him to rebuy antidepressant pills, which was seen as embarrassing, paternalistic, and an intrusion on privacy.
- A senior vice president of a taxi providing service threatened that it had records on personal lives of journalists who dared to write critically about the company.

It is easy to get carried away by the promise of data-based marketing. It is indeed a powerful tool, but just that—a tool for the help of humans. It cannot solve all problems of understanding consumers; ultimately a human will have to see how it can be used. Customer relationships cannot be reduced to a set of numbers, but it is also important to understand cultural and emotional bonds as well. Brands have to try to build love, as Kevin Roberts writes, which can be done by a combination of online and offline methods, and that is where the real role of marketing comes in. "That requires understanding customers as people—nuanced, dynamic, unpredictable—not just collections of data," write Lee and Sobol.

Also, the future may not be so connected after all. An alternative scenario is that people realize the dangers of misuse of online data and the loss of privacy—and begin to switch off. This becomes plausible if data is hacked in a big way and people are harmed as a result. If sometime in the future, a large number of people suffer because of leakage of data, it is quite possible that they begin to switch off. It is not such a distant prophecy—already some people are deleting their social media profiles.

However, it would be quite difficult to switch off from the addictive power of the Internet. The advance of technology offers another scenario as well. Davenport and Kirby (2015) write that automation has taken away much of the drudge work from humans; artificial intelligence is taking away decision-making work also. As a consequence, more jobs will be taken away by machines. "Unless we find as many tasks to give humans as we find to take away from them, all the social and psychological ills of joblessness will grow, from economic recession to youth unemployment to individual crises of identity," they write. Human civilization may well see a future of jobless growth. If large parts of the population are economically disadvantaged, will we see a society firmly divided into haves and have-nots? This scenario may well be somewhat like the dystopia described in Suzanne Collins' *The Hunger Games*. In the books, *Panem* is a country with a wealthy Capitol and 12 districts living in poverty. Will our world look like Panem in the future?

A Faustian Bargain

It is a *Brave New World* with a difference—here the objective is to know the needs of customers and sell to them. Consumers are happy that they get things even before they want them. But it is also a Faustian bargain: while people are happy to shop and transact, companies get ever more data that is farmed from consumers' online activities and sensors to track every aspect of their lives.

And this also tempts governments, terrorists, hackers, and other groups—why not use all this data to control or subjugate populations?

As Schmidt and Cohen (2013) explain, "The impact of data revolution will be to strip citizens of much of their control over their personal information in virtual space, and that will have significant consequences in the physical world." The potential for someone to access and manipulate our online identities will increase. Every online activity will be tracked and regulated by the government. It is like living in a glass bowl, where every action is visible, every movement analyzed. "As smart-phones become loaded with ever more sensors, and with software that can interpret their users' emotional states, the scope for manipulating minds is growing," cautions *The Economist* (January 3, 2015).

As a consequence, there is the possibility that consumers will start feeling uncomfortable with the kind of information that they share online. It is likely that people start fretting about the limits of privacy. In addition, there is the real fear that data that people share online can be misused for ulterior motives.

Misuse of Data

Very accurate customer profiles provided by big data analysis tell us about people and their behavior, but also are open for misuse. They contain thousands of pieces of data that accurately describe the socioeconomic and ethnic profiles of people, along with their habits and psychology. Some companies have profiles on millions of consumers, which are used to categorize people into precise segments. "This application of big data technology, if used improperly, irresponsibly, or nefariously, could have significant ramifications for targeted individuals," says a White House report (2014), highlighting the threat that big data poses.

Data can be misused in various ways as follows:

- By using algorithms and getting information that is more accurate than traditional credit scores, consumers can be denied credit, employment, or other benefits. The information may be generated for marketing purposes, but can also be used to influence individuals' opportunities to find housing, job opportunities, or find out the future health of applicants. For instance, a person's past history is available in detail in pictures and comments they made on their social media sites.

- The data can be used to label populations on some characteristics which can lead to discrimination. For instance, *The Wall Street Journal* (2012) found that some retailers use an algorithm to generate different discounts for the same product to people based on location: People in higher-income areas received higher discounts than people in lower-income areas. Individuals can also be classified to enable discrimination and reinforce social stratification.
- The fight against terrorism gives enormous powers to governments to collect data about individuals. Movements of people are tracked secretly by the government monitoring their mobile phone records, e-mails, and social media. This data can easily be misused by dictators or even democratically elected governments for nefarious ends; it could also fall in the hands of criminal organizations or a future dictator.
- Loopholes in social media sites and cloud storage have resulted in the release of private pictures of celebrities and other people. Ordinary people too can find their deeply personal data hacked and posted publicly.
- Internet companies frequently bypass the privacy settings of people without their knowledge or consent. Apps transmit personal identifying details to tracking companies.
- Companies can increase insurance rates by using genetic data for people who may have the possibility of getting a certain disease in the future.
- Big data analysis gives powers of predictive policing: It helps in knowing the likelihood of a crime before it is committed, based on the likelihoods analyzed by data analysis. Would it also lead to imprisoning or surveillance of people based on their likelihood of committing a crime in the future?

The real danger is racial profiling: The personal data can be misused by the government or criminal organizations for ulterior motives. "The history of the 20th century is blood soaked with situations in which data abetted ugly ends," write Mayer-Schönberger and Cukier (2013). They give the example of invading Nazis, who used civil records in the

Netherlands to round up Jews. "The five-digit numbers tattooed into the forearms of Nazi concentration camp prisoners initially corresponded to IBM Hollerith punch card numbers; data processing facilities facilitated murder on an industrial scale," they write.

The difference now is that data available is much more in quantity and much better in targeting individuals. Even the movement of people can be tracked today. Social data and algorithmic models can predict which people are likely to be dissidents.

Though it is shocking, the digitally connected age also means the age of constant surveillance. Our e-mails, phone records, social data—and practically everything we do—are being watched.

Dixon and Gellman (2014) in their report, *The Scoring of America*, write that scores are being calculated for all citizens. "New consumer scores use thousands of pieces of information about consumers' pasts to predict how they will behave in the future," they write. People do not know what aspects of their behavior are being scored and how those scores will be used. *Consumers who do not know about the existence or use of consumer scores cannot have any say in who used the scores, or how.*

Whether people remain comfortable with the complete loss of their privacy or whether the backlash against big data gathers momentum, however, remains to be seen. The future is another country. A possible scenario is that people remain connected but learn to safeguard their personal data. They only share the data when they need to and only with companies that promise complete security. Perhaps that is more plausible. Or, the future is something we have not imagined so far and we must wait to find out how the connected consumer evolves. What shape Big Brother takes remains to be seen.

References

Abbruzzese, J.Y. May 9, 2014. "Why CNN Is Obsessed With Flight 370: 'The Audience Has Spoken.'" http://mashable.com/2014/05/09/cnn-obsessed-malaysia-mh370-zucker/

Adler, E. 2014. "Reverse Showrooming: Bricks-And-Mortar Retailers Fight Back." *Business Insider*, February 14. http://www.businessinsider.in/Reverse-Showrooming-Bricks-And-Mortar-Retailers-Fight-Back/articleshow/30411064.cms

Aljukhadar, M., and S. Senecal. 2011. "Segmenting the Online Consumer Market." *Marketing Intelligence & Planning* 29, no. 4, pp. 421–435.

Aubrey, C., and D. Judge. April–June 2012. "Re-Imagine Retail: Why Store Innovation is Key to a Brand's Growth in the 'New Normal', Digitally-Connected and Transparent World." *Journal of Brand Strategy* 1, no. 1, pp. 31–39.

Audi. 2014. http://www.audi.co.uk/audi-innovation/audi-city.html (accessed December 12)

Barton, D., and D. Court. October 2012. "Making Advanced Analytics Work for You." *Harvard Business Review*, pp. 78–83.

Bell, D. 2014. *Location Is (Still) Everything: The Surprising Influence of the Real World on How We Search, Shop, and Sell in the Virtual One*. Seattle: Amazon Publishing.

Berger, J. 2013. *Contagious: Why Things Catch On*. New York: Simon & Schuster.

Berman, S.J. 2012. "Digital Transformation: Opportunities to Create New Business Models." *Strategy & Leadership* 40, no. 2, pp. 18–24.

Bernhard, R., and A. Olderog. 2014. "The Changing Role of the CMO." Vivaldi Partners.

Blank, S. August 8, 2014. "Know Your Customers by Living a Day in Their Lives." *Entrepreneur*. http://www.entrepreneur.com/article/236301

Brown, S. October 2001. "Torment Your Customers (They'll Love It)." *Harvard Business Review*.

Bughin, J., J. Doogan, and O.J. Vetvik. April 2010. "A New Way to Measure Word-of-Mouth Marketing." *McKinsey Quarterly*. http://www.mckinsey.com/insights/marketing_sales/a_new_way_to_measure_word-of-mouth_marketing

Business Standard. April 16, 2015. "Is India in an E-commerce Bubble?" http://www.business-standard.com/article/companies/is-india-in-an-e-commerce-bubble-115041600253_1.html

Carter, B. 2014. "CNN's Ratings Surge Covering the Mystery of the Missing Airliner." *The New York Times*, March 17. http://www.nytimes.com/2014/03/18/business/media/cnns-ratings-surge-with-coverage-of-the-mystery-of-the-missing-airliner.html?_r=0

Chaffey, D. 2009. *E-commerce and E-commerce Management*. 4th ed. Essex: Pearson Education.

CISCO Internet Business Solutions Group. May 2011. "Unifying Customer Experience in a Multichannel World: Unlocking the Full Potential of Multiple Channels To Engage, Acquire, and Retain Customers." http://www.cisco.com/web/about/ac79/docs/innov/Multichannel-Customer-Experience_IBSG_0519.pdf

Claessens, S., T. Glaessner, and D. Klingebiel. June 2001. "E-Finance in Emerging Markets: Is Leapfrogging Possible?" *World Bank Financial Sector Discussion Paper No. 7*. http://www1.worldbank.org/finance/assets/images/E-Finance_ii.pdf

Clifford, S. 2012. "Malls' New Pitch: Come for the Experience." *The New York Times*, July 17.

Court, D. August 2007. "The Evolving role of the CMO." *McKinsey Quarterly*.

Court, D., D. Elzinga, S. Mulder, and O.J. Vetvik. June 2009. "The Consumer Decision Journey." *McKinsey Quarterly* 3, pp. 96–107.

Court, D., J. Gordon, and J. Perrey. May 2012. "Measuring Marketing's Worth." *McKinsey Quarterly*. http://www.mckinsey.com/insights/marketing_sales/measuring_marketings_worth (accessed December 12, 2014).

Davenport, T.H. January 2006. "Competing on Analytics." *Harvard Business Review*.

Davenport, T.H. 2014. *Big Data at Work: Dispelling the Myths, Uncovering the Opportunities*. Boston: Harvard Business Press Books.

Davenport, T.H. December 2013. "Analytics 3.0." *Harvard Business Review*.

Davenport, T.H., and J. Kirby. June 2015. "Beyond Automation." *Harvard Business Review*.

Davenport, T.H., L.D. Mule, and J. Lucker. December 2011. "Know What Your Customers Want Before They Do." *Harvard Business Review*.

Dixon, P., and R. Gellman. April 2014. "The Scoring of America: How Secret Consumer Scores Threaten Your Privacy and Your Future." *World Privacy Forum* http://www.worldprivacyforum.org/wp-content/uploads/2014/04/WPF_Scoring_of_America_April2014_fs.pdf

Duhigg, C. 2012. "How Companies Learn Your Secrets." *The New York Times*, February 16. http://www.nytimes.com/2012/02/19/magazine/shopping-habits.html

Eagle Eye. (n.d.). www.eagleye.com

Economist Intelligence Unit (EIU). 2007. "Beyond Loyalty: Meeting the Challenge of Customer Engagement Part I." *The Economist Intelligence Unit.* http://www.adobe.com/engagement/pdfs/partI.pdf

Ernst and Young. (n.d). What's Next for Business? Six Global Trends. http://www.ey.com/GL/en/Issues/Business-environment/Business-redefined---Global-trend-1--the-rise-and-rise-of-emerging-markets

The Economist. 2011. "Print Me a Stradivarius." February 10.

The Economist. 2012. "Collaborative Manufacturing: All Together Now." April 21.

The Economist. 2013a. "Every Step You Take." November 16.

The Economist. 2013b. "Secrets, Lies and America's Spies." June 15.

The Economist. 2014. "Biometrics: Clocking People's Clocks." August 23.

The Economist. 2015. "Getting Hooked." January 3.

Edelman, D.C. December 2010. "Branding in the Digital Age." *Harvard Business Review* 88, no. 12, pp. 62–69.

Ettenson, R., E. Conrado, and J. Knowles. January 2013. "Rethinking the 4Ps." *Harvard Business Review.*

Farris, P.W., N.T. Bendle, P.E. Pfeifer, and D.J. Reibstein. 2006. *Marketing Metrics: 50+ Metrics Every Executive Should Master.* Upper Saddle River, NJ: Pearson Education.

Fields, R. 2014. "Four Forces Driving Contemporary Culture Deeper Into the Organization." *Forbes CMO Network.* http://www.forbes.com/sites/onmarketing/2014/06/30/four-forces-driving-contemporary-culture-deeper-into-the-organization/

Fields, R. June 2014. "Four Forces Driving Contemporary Culture Deeper into the Organization." *Forbes CMO Network.* http://www.forbes.com/sites/onmarketing/2014/06/30/four-forces-driving-contemporary-culture-deeper-into-the-organization/

Fournier, S., and L. Lee. April 2009. "Getting Brand Communities Right." *Harvard Business Review.*

Frelin, J. 2013. "The Digital Disruption of Marketing and the Executive Knowledge Gap." *Bloomberg Business week*, October 7.

Garfield, B. 2009. *The Chaos Scenario.* Nashville, TN: Stielstra Publishing.

Gartner Group. February 13, 2014. "Press Release: Gartner Says Annual Smartphone Sales Surpassed Sales of Feature Phones for the First Time in 2013." http://www.gartner.com/newsroom/id/2665715

Giamanco, B., and K. Gregoire. July–August 2012. "Tweet Me, Friend Me, Make Me Buy." *Harvard Business Review.*

Google and Ad Age. February 2014. "Brand Engagement in Participation Age." https://think.storage.googleapis.com/docs/brand-engagement-in-participation-age_research-studies.pdf

Greenberg, P. 2010. *CRM at the Speed of Light*. 4th ed. New York: McGraw Hill.

Gregg, B., W. Maes, and A. Pickersgill. June 2014. "Marketing's Age of Relevance: How to Read and React to Customer Signals." McKinsey and Co.

Gulati, R., and J. Garino. May 2000. "Get the Right Mix of Bricks and Clicks." *Harvard Business Review*.

Hagen, P. February 2011. "The Rise of the Chief Customer Officer." http://www.forbes.com/2011/02/10/chief-customer-officer-leadership-cmo-network-rise.html

How People Really Use Mobile. January–February 2013. *Harvard Business Review*.

Hudspeth, N. April–June, 2012. "Building a Brand Socially." *Journal of Brand Strategy* 1, no. 1, pp. 25–30.

IBM (n.d.). http://www-03.ibm.com/press/us/en/presskit/27297.wss

Kadlec, D. 2012. "How Smart Phones Are Changing the Way We Bank, Drive, Have Sex and Go to the Bathroom." *Time*, June 22. http://business.time.com/2012/06/22/how-smart-phones-are-changing-the-way-we-bank-and-drive/

Kalyanam, K., and M. Zweben. November 2005. "The Perfect Message at the Perfect Moment." *Harvard Business Review*.

Kanter Retail. 2013. The Future Shopper. http://uk.kantar.com/media/356202/fp_the_future_shopper_march_2013_-_final.pdf

Kanter, R.M. January 2001. "The Ten Deadly Mistakes of Wanna-Dots." *Harvard Business Review*, pp. 91–100.

Keiningham, T.L., L. Aksoy, A. Buoye, and B. Cooil. October 2011. "Customer Loyalty isn't Enough. Grow Your Share of Wallet." *Harvard Business Review*.

Kohn, S. March 25, 2014. "Why are We So Obsessed with Flight 370?" http://edition.cnn.com/2014/03/19/opinion/kohn-flight-370-obsession/

Kumar, D. 2012. *Marketing Channels*. New Delhi: Oxford University Press.

Kumar, V., L. Aksoy, B. Donkers, R. Venkatesan, T. Wiesel, and S. Tillmanns. 2010. "Undervalued or Overvalued Customers: Capturing Total Customer Engagement Value." *Journal of Service Research* 13, no. 3, pp. 297–310.

Kumar, V., V. Chattaraman, C. Neghina, B. Skiera, L. Aksoy, A. Buoye, and J. Henseler. 2013. "Data-Driven Services Marketing in a Connected World." *Journal of Service Management* 24, no. 3, pp. 330–52.

Lecinski, J. 2011. "Winning the Zero Moment of Truth," *Google Inc.* http://www.thinkwithgoogle.com/collections/zero-moment-truth.html

Lee, B. August 2012. "Marketing Is Dead." *HBR Blog Network*. http://blogs.hbr.org/2012/08/marketing-is-dead/

Lee, L., and D. Sobol. August 27, 2012. "What Data Can't Tell You About Customers." *HBR Blog Network*. http://blogs.hbr.org/2012/08/what-data-cant-tell-you-about/

Lindsay, K. September 9, 2014. "Why Your Marketing Metrics Don't Add Up." *HBR Blog Network*. http://blogs.hbr.org/2014/09/why-your-marketing-metrics-dont-add-up/

Loveman, G.W. May 2003. "Diamonds in the Data Mine." *Harvard Business Review*.

Macy's Annual Report. 2013. https://www.macysinc.com/for-investors/annual-report/archives/default.aspx

Mayer-Schönberger, V., and K. Cukier. 2013. *Big Data: A Revolution That Will Transform How We Live, Work, and Think*. London: John Murray.

McAfee, A., and E. Brynjolfsson. October 2012. "Big Data: The Management Revolution." *Harvard Business Review*.

McGuire T., C. Meyer, and D. Stone. October 2013. "The Data-Driven Life." McKinsey and Co. http://www.mckinseyonmarketingandsales.com/the-data-driven-life

McKinsey & Co. May. 2012. "Minding Your Digital Business: McKinsey Global Survey Results" http://www.mckinsey.com/insights/business_technology/minding_your_digital_business_mckinsey_global_survey_results

McKinsey and Co. December 2012. "The Marketing Organization of the Future." http://mckinseyonmarketingandsales.com/the-marketing-organization-of-the-future

McKinsey Global Institute. March 2013. "China's E-tail Revolution." http://www.mckinsey.com/insights/asia-pacific/china_e-tailing

McWilliam, G. 2000. "Building Stronger Brands through Online Communities." *MIT Sloan Management Review*.

Meer, D. 2014. "When Big Data Isn't an Option." *Strategy+Business*. Issue 75, Summer 2014.

Millward Brown. 2013. *Marketing 2020*. https://www.millwardbrown.com/docs/default-source/optimor-downloads/marketing-2020.pdf?sfvrsn=2

Moran, G., L. Muzellec, and E. Nolan. 2014. "Consumer Moments of Truth in the Digital Context: How 'Search' and 'E-Word of Mouth' Can Fuel Consumer Decision-Making." *Journal of Advertising Research* 54, no. 2 pp. 200-04.

Mutiga, M. 2014. "Kenya's Banking Revolution Lights a Fire." *The New York Times*, January 20. http://www.nytimes.com/2014/01/21/opinion/kenyas-banking-revolution-lights-a-fire.html?_r=0

Nielsen. 2012. "How Digital Influences How We Shop Around the World." http://www.nielsen.com/us/en/insights/reports/2012/how-digital-influences-how-we-shop-around-the-world.html

Nielsen and NM Incite's U.S. Digital Consumer Report. 2012. http://www.nielsen.com/us/en/insights/news/2012/introducing-generation-c.html

Nielsen. 2014. "The US Digital Consumer Report." http://www.nielsen.com/us/en/insights/reports/2014/the-us-digital-consumer-report.html

Oracle White Paper. September 2011. "The Future of Retail: Through the Eyes of Digital Natives."

Pasquale, F. 2014. *The Black Box Society: The Secret Algorithm Behind Money and Information*. Boston: Harvard University Press.

Pearson, T.R. 2011. *The Old Rules Of Market Are Dead*. New Delhi: Tata McGraw Hill.

Pentland, A. 2014. *Social Physics: How Good Ideas Spread—The Lessons from a New Science*. New York: Penguin Press.

Pine, B.J., and K.C. Korn. 2011. *Infinite Possibility: Creating Customer Value on the Digital Frontier*. 1st ed. San Francisco, CA: Berrett-Koehler Publishers, Inc.

Piskorsk, M.J. November 2011. "Social Strategies That Work." *Harvard Business Review*.

Porter, M. March 2001. "Strategy and the Internet." *Harvard Business Review*.

Porter, M.E., and J.E. Heppelmann. November 2014. "How Smart, Connected Products Are Transforming Competition." *Harvard Business Review*.

Prahalad, C.K., and V. Ramaswamy. 2004. *The Future of Competition: Co-creating Unique Experiences with Customers*. Boston: Harvard Business School Press.

Rangaswamy, A., and G. Van Bruggen. 2015. "Opportunities and Challenges in Multichannel Marketing: An Introduction to the Special Issue." *Journal of Interactive Marketing* 19, no. 2, pp. 5–11.

Rayport J.F. March 1, 2013. "Advertising and the Internet of Things." *HBR Blog Network*. https://hbr.org/2013/03/advertising-and-the-internet-o/

Rayport J.F. March 2013. "Advertising's New Medium: Human Experience." *Harvard Business Review*.

Regalado, A. November 4, 2013. "It's All E-Commerce Now." *MIT Technology Review*.http://www.technologyreview.com/news/520786/its-all-e-commerce-now/

Reichheld, F.F., and P. Schefter. July-August 2000. "E-Loyalty: Your Secret Weapon on the Web." *Harvard Business Review*.

Retail 2020: Reinventing Retailing—Once Again. January 2012. IBM. http://www-01.ibm.com/common/ssi/cgi-bin/ssialias?infotype=SA&subtype=WH&htmlfid=REW03013USEN

Rigby, D. December 2011. "The Future of Shopping." *Harvard Business Review*.

Roberts, K. 2004. *Lovemarks*. New York: Powerhouse Books.

Ross, J.W., C.M. Beath, and A. Quaadgras. December 2013. "You May Not Need Big Data After All." *Harvard Business Review*.

Rust, R.T., C. Moorman, and G. Bhalla. January 2010. "Rethinking Marketing." *Harvard Business Review*.

Rutkin. A. April 17, 2014. "Wikipedia Searches and Sick Tweets Predict Flu cases." *New Scientist.* http://www.newscientist.com/article/dn25435-wikipedia-searches-and-sick-tweets-predict-flu-cases.html#.VXggF9Kqqko

Schadler, T., J. Bernoff, and J. Ask. 2014. *The Mobile Mind Shift: Engineer Your Business to Win in the Mobile Moment.* Cambridge, MA: Groundswell Press.

Schloss, J. October 14, 2014. "Big Data's Dark Side: Keep the Creep Out of Your Analytics." CMS Wire. http://www.cmswire.com/cms/digital-marketing/big-datas-dark-side-keep-the-creep-out-of-your-analytics-026817.php (accessed December 12, 2014).

Schmitt, B. 2012. "The Consumer Psychology of Brands." *Journal of Consumer Psychology* 22, no. 1, pp. 7–17.

Schmidt, E., and J. Cohen. 2013. *The New Digital Age: Reshaping the Future of People, Nations and Business.* London: John Murray.

Sehgal, V. 2013. "Forrester Research Online Retail Forecast, 2013 To 2018 (US)." Forrester Research. http://www.forrester.com/Forrester+Research+Online+Retail+Forecast+2013+To+2018+US/fulltext/-/E-RES115941

Seven Shades of Mobile. October 2012. https://advertising.aol.com/sites/advertising.aol.com/files/insights/research-reports/downloads/aol-bbdo-7-shades-mobile-abstract-final.pdf

Seybold P.B. May 2001. "Get Inside the Lives of Your Customers." *Harvard Business Review.*

Simonson, I., and E. Rosen. 2014. *Absolute Value.* New York: Harper Business.

Sklar, C. February 2014. "The Traditional CMO Role is Dead: Long Live the Chief Customer Officer." *The Guardian Blog.* http://www.theguardian.com/media-network/media-network-blog/2014/feb/19/cmo-role-dead-customer-officer-engagement

Solis, B. 2012. *The End of Business as Usual.* NJ: John Wiley and Sons.

Sorce, P., V. Perotti, and S. Widrick. 2005. "Attitude and Age Differences in Online Buying." *International Journal of Retail and Distribution Management* 33, no. 2, pp. 122–32.

Spaulding, E., and C. Perry. September 16, 2013. "Making it Personal: Rules for Success in Product Customization." *Bain and Co.* http://www.bain.com/publications/articles/making-it-personal-rules-for-success-in-product-customization.aspx

Stauffer, J. April–June 2012. "Social Brand Planning." *Journal of Brand Strategy* 1, no. 1, pp. 40–49.

Strauss, J., and R. Frost. 2012. *E-Marketing.* 6th ed. Boston: Pearson Education.

The Guardian Media Network Blog. 2013. Apple iBeacons: What are They and What Do They Mean for Retail? November 11. http://www.theguardian.com/media-network/media-network-blog/2013/nov/11/apple-ibeacons-retail

Thomasson, E. October 26, 2012. "Insight—At Nestle, Interacting with the Online Enemy." Reuters. http://uk.reuters.com/article/2012/10/26/uk-nestle-online-water-idUKBRE89P07Q20121026

Time. 2012. "How Smart Phones Are Changing the Way We Bank, Drive, Have Sex and Go to the Bathroom." June 22. http://business.time.com/2012/06/22/how-smart-phones-are-changing-the-way-we-bank-and-drive/#ixzz2CXJ1HOQt

Time. 2014. "Here's Proof You're More Addicted to Your Phone (and Tablet) Than Ever." April 22. http://time.com/73033/mobile-addiction-rising/

Todd, P. 2014. "Blurring the Lines Between Online and High Street Shopping." *The Guardian*, October 28. http://www.theguardian.com/media-network-partner-zone-ebay/2014/oct/28/blurring-lines-online-high-street-shopping

Treacy, M., and F. Wiersema. 1995. *The Discipline of Market Leaders: Choose Your Customers, Narrow Your Focus, Dominate Your Market*. Reading, MA: Addison-Wesley Publishing Co.

Tufekci, Z., and B. King. 2014. "We Can't Trust Uber." *The New York Times*. December 7. http://www.nytimes.com/2014/12/08/opinion/we-cant-trust-uber.html?_r=0 (accessed December 8, 2014).

Valentino-Devries, J., J. Singer-Vine, and A. Soltani. December 24, 2012. "Websites Vary Prices, Deals Based on Users' In-formation." *The Wall Street Journal*. http://online.wsj.com/articles/SB10001424127887323777204578189391813881534 (accessed December 12, 2014).

Vivaldi Partners. February 13, 2014. "The Always on Consumer." http://vivaldipartners.com/pdf/VPG_Always-On%20Consumer%20Study%202014.pdf

Webster, F.E. and R.F. Lusch. 2013. "Elevating Marketing: Marketing Is Dead! Long Live Marketing!" *Journal of the Academy of Market Science* 41, pp. 389–99.

White House Report. May 2014. *Big Data: Seizing Opportunities, Preserving Values*. The White House. www.WhiteHouse.gov/BigData

Wind, Y. Summer 2008. "A Plan to Invent the Marketing We Need Today." *MIT Sloan Management Review*.

Index

CPSIA information can be obtained
at www.ICGtesting.com
Printed in the USA
BVOW11s0821010817

490806BV00006B/29/P